MATCH
OF MY LIFE

T0150653

MATCH
OF MY LIFE

Sixteen stars relive their greatest games

Stoke City

Simon Lowe

This edition first published by Pitch Publishing 2012

Pitch Publishing
A2 Yeoman Gate
Yeoman Way
Durrington
BN13 3QZ
www.pitchpublishing.co.uk

A CIP catalogue record is available for this book
from the British Library

ISBN 978-1-9080517-6-9

Typesetting and origination by Pitch Publishing.

Printed in India by Replika Press Pvt. Ltd.

Acknowledgements

Thanks to John Booth, Tony Scholes and Peter Coates at Stoke City FC for giving this project their full backing. It would not have been possible without the contact books of Terry Conroy, who does know just about everybody in football and Brendan O'Callaghan. The response from the players who have taken part in this book has been remarkable. I hope they had as much fun reliving their greatest moments as I did.

A big thank you must go to Roger Martin for allowing me the run of his phenomenal programme collection, Julian Boodell and Andy Peck for assistance with photographs and the Sports Department of the Sentinel, especially Keith Wales, who have ably assisted me when it came to finding photographs and providing publicity for this book. Many thanks go to Bury FC for the hospitality shown to me while visiting them to interview Mike Sheron and Peter Fox.

I would also like to mention several players who wished to contribute to this book, but who couldn't because of circumstance or time constraints. Eric Skeels, Stoke's record appearance holder, had an illness in the family, while Adrian Heath had the misfortune to be made caretaker-manager at Coventry City after the departure of Micky Adams and his duties meant he was unable to take part too. Steve Bould, John Mahoney, Paul Bracewell, Lee Sandford and Alan Hudson all also would have loved to take part, but logistics rendered it impossible. Maybe they will all be available to help should another volume of great memories be judged a good idea!

Simon Lowe

This book is dedicated to Sir Stanley Matthews.
Stoke-on-Trent's greatest son and greatest inspiration.

Contents

Introduction

I sat in the Crown Inn at Betley, on the Crewe road, opposite one of Stoke's greatest ever goalkeepers. He showed me the hands that had been gnarled by years of catching the heavy, sodden, leather ball, and the scars from the explosion as the shell ripped through his tank in Northern France.

Dennis Herod was a hero to many during Stoke's tilt at the 1946/47 League Championship – the closest City have ever come to winning the title – but not too many fans even then knew the full story behind his incredible resurrection from war invalid to goalkeeping legend. And even if they did, it wasn't that unusual – there had been a war on.

The tears rolled down Dennis's cheeks as he recounted to me tales of his fellow players from that team – all now, following the death of Frank Mountford in 2006, departed. When I asked him to choose his favourite, or best game for the club, he immediately told me that there was only one game that really mattered – the one which would have seen Stoke win the league title in June 1947. Defeat to Sheffield United cost City that accolade, but Dennis still recalls it vividly despite the crushing disappointment, just as he remembered the players and friends he had cherished during his time at Stoke. He was recalling the good old days, of course, with rose-tinted spectacles, naturally, but he captured for me the spirit of playing football for a living and an era when the true reward for the players was the passion of pulling on the shirt and the glory of winning.

Back in the 1940s players were true working class heroes, living amongst the communities that they represented wholeheartedly on a Saturday afternoon, travelling to the game on the same bus or tram and drinking in the same pubs. Even until the 1970s, and the era of Hudson, Greenhoff and Smith, that remained true, although the likes of George Best had begun to lift top footballers into the realms of superstardom. Nowadays, of course, even a common or garden player makes far more cash than the average fan, and lives an aloof life. They still represent us out on the pitch, but it's not quite the same. Whether you think that's because of the money that's come into the game, or the move to the new, slightly sterile modern ground, the birth of Sky TV, or a combination of all those things, the irrevocable fact is, it ain't like it used to be.

The one Match Of My Life chapter that I would truly liked to have recorded is that of Sir Stanley Matthews. Having been fortunate enough to meet the great man on a number of occasions and also having interviewed him several times, I talked with Stan about many great matches in which he performed heroics for Stoke. He was particularly fond of the 3-1 victory over Chelsea in 1934 in the fifth round of the FA Cup, a game in which he scored two goals; "I was a bit of a goalscorer back in those days!" he told me in that self-effacing way of his.

He also spoke glowingly of a 0-0 draw with the great Herbert Chapman Arsenal team, including his own personal hero Alex James, on Easter Saturday 1937; a match which attracted the largest ever crowd to the Victoria Ground of 51,373. But my feeling is that, despite occasions such as his incredible comeback match in October 1961 against Huddersfield, which effectively revitalised the club, and the 1962/63 promotion-clinching victory over Luton in which Stan scored, relived in this book by goalkeeper Jimmy O'Neill, the game which meant the most to him was his farewell match in which Stoke played a team assembled from global superstars such as Puskas, Di Stefano, Masopust and Yashin. The match was beamed to a worldwide audience of 112 million people – in those days Stoke City FC were big news.

Stan always spoke about how he was honoured by the way these great players had come to Stoke to support him and how the public had turned out to bid him a teary farewell. Typically he never wanted to take the limelight, or boast about his personal achievement, but that night just allowed him a doff of his metaphoric cap in acknowledgment as he was chaired off the field to wild applause.

This book is dedicated to the memory of Sir Stan, whose presence lives on in the form of the Sir Stanley Matthews Foundation which does such good work around the Potteries encouraging children to get involved in sport. One pound from the sale of each copy of this book will be donated to the Foundation, whose chairman,

BBC Radio Stoke's commentator Nigel Johnson, also provides the Foreword.

All the Stoke heroes who have contributed to this book have shown, in their own way, what an indelible mark the club has left upon them. The spread of legends taking part means that the book covers 60 years of Stoke City matches; the era may change, but always the pride and passion shine through.

Of course all supporters have their own favourite Stoke game. It's always a match that has that special meaning for them personally. Mine would probably be the 4-3 victory over West Brom in September 1992 which sparked the club record unbeaten run that would finally see Lou Macari's team win the Division Two title. But I'd also have a strong word for the two Wembley wins of 1992 and 2000.

The reasons each player has for selecting their favourite game are many and varied. Denis Smith loved pitting his wits against the greatest club side in the world in Ajax in the mid-1970s, Paul Maguire couldn't better his debut, even with that famous four goal performance against Wolves which saved Stoke from relegation in 1984, Mark Stein and Brendan O'Callaghan both preferred defeating Manchester United to their respective promotion triumphs, goalkeeper Peter Fox strangely chose a match in which he was sent off (!) and only played 28 minutes, while, perhaps more predictably, Terry Conroy just had to choose his goal at Wembley which helped Stoke win the 1972 League Cup.

Inevitably it was more difficult to track down the modern players, who are still either in the game playing at other clubs, or who coach. This means that the book does not feature a chapter by James O'Connor for example, about his incredible night at Ninian Park that saw Stoke through to the 2002 play-off final and ultimately promotion. I chased Peter Thorne and Peter Hoekstra to, but to no avail. I would love to be able to put that right one day.

There was plenty of incident along the way. Tony Allen's wife misheard part of my phone conversation arranging a time to meet him for a pint in the Barlaston Inn, and thought he was arranging to elope! Both Tony and I agreed that we were past that sort of thing.

Getting any kind of sense out of Don Ratcliffe and Johnny King when they are together with a pint in their hands is easier said than done, while the extreme January weather severly hampered my trek around the Manchester area where several of the heroes who contributed to the book now reside.

Then I came across Ian Painter, who I discovered is still recovering from the terrible shock of suffering a stroke at the age of 41. Worried about what he might actually be able to remember about his chosen match against Liverpool in 1984, Ian was very nervous in agreeing to an interview. But the memories flooded back and he felt that the experience had been extremely cathartic for him and helped give him confidence in continuing his recuperation. I am delighted that reliving his greatest Stoke moments may have played some part in helping him recover.

But wherever I went and whoever I met, I was always greeted with tales of playing for the great club that is Stoke City Football Club and how much that honour meant to each of these players.

Witnessing Dennis Herod's tears allowed me to reflect on the other side of football, which fans are often not privy to. The camaraderie of the dressing room – so often cited as what a professional player misses the most when time forces him to give up the game – clearly has left an indelible mark on so many of these men.

The pride and passion they showed on the pitch whilst wearing the red and white stripes and also when speaking to me years later about their magic moments, glowed through like a beacon. Stoke fans love players who really care about the club and demonstrate that wholeheartedly on the pitch and we've been lucky to have many of those who also had a great deal of talent over the years.

The club's history is such a vital part of why Stoke City is a great footballing name and I hope this book reflects at least some of the great games and great players who have kept us royally entertained over the years and informs and entertains all Stoke fans, whatever their age.

Simon Lowe

Foreword

by Nigel Johnson

THERE ARE NOT many youngsters who enjoy football that haven't dreamed of becoming a professional footballer. Fifty or sixty years ago it wasn't for the money because the footballer earned similar wages to the spectators on the terraces. Many travelled to the game on public transport and chatted with supporters on the way to the match.

How different it is today. The lure of the lucrative contract that will make a player secure for the rest of his life is a big incentive, but being able to perform in front of thousands of adoring fans is a bonus as well. Many players over the decades have said how fortunate they have been to be paid to do something that they enjoy so much. Every player has memories etched in the mind and in this book Simon Lowe has encapsulated the great moments enjoyed by a number of former players from Dennis Herod in the 1940s to Mike Sheron in the 1990s.

I have watched Stoke City for 50 years. At first I stood at the Town End or in the Butler Street paddock, but from the '70s I have been privileged to cover Stoke's games from the press box for BBC Radio Stoke. My profession was teaching, but I have been fortunate to have been involved with broadcasting sport in parallel with my teaching career.

There have been some magical moments along the way. The first game that I remember was in February 1948 at the Victoria Ground. Arsenal were the visitors and there were 45,000 thronging the ground that day and they witnessed a goalless draw. I don't recall anything of the game itself, but was fascinated as a little boy sitting on my father's shoulders listening to the roaring supporters and the crackling rattles.

There were interesting games throughout the '50s, but it was the return of Stanley Matthews in 1961 that set the supporters' pulses racing. The team was heading for relegation to the Third Division until he arrived, but he transformed the performances and brought a broad smile to the face of manager Tony Waddington.

The 18th May 1963 saw Luton Town come to the Victoria Ground for the last home game of the season. Over 33,000 attended because Stoke needed a win to gain promotion to the First Division (now the Premiership). Jackie Mudie opened the scoring for Stoke, but the second goal brought the house down. Jimmy McIlroy slid a ball to Stanley Matthews just inside the Luton half. Stan controlled the ball and began to glide forwards leaving Luton players in his wake. As he entered the penalty area he rounded the outcoming goalkeeper and slotted the ball home in front of the Boothen End. The roar could be heard in Hanley. The Potters were promoted and the Wizard of Dribble had secured the success.

This fabulous game is relived in this book by Jimmy O'Neill, Stoke's goalkeeper that fateful day, while Don Ratcliffe and Tony Allen also recall games from the tail end of the crucial promotion season.

Two years later, in 1965, on a late April evening, Stanley Matthews bade farewell to the game he had enriched for over 33 years and football stars from across the globe came to honour one of the greatest players to have graced the game. It was a fantastic night and tears rolled down my cheeks at the end as I rose from my seat in the Butler Street stand as Stanley was chaired from the packed arena on the shoulders of Russian goalkeeper Lev Yashin and the Hungarian genius Ferenc Puskas. Little did I know that 35 years later, following Sir Stan's death, I would be asked to form the Sir Stanley Matthews Foundation.

Although I was covering City games in 1972 for BBC Radio Stoke, I was not part of the team covering the League Cup Final in March. I bought my ticket and revelled in Chelsea's demise as Conroy and Eastham supplied the goals which won the match. What a moment when Peter Dobing lifted the cup aloft. A major trophy at last for the Potters as Terry Conroy remembers with his own very personal recollections of that triumphant day.

Twenty years later Stoke were back at Wembley for the Autoglass Final against Stockport County. I commentated on the game from a box just to the right of the Royal Box. Mark Stein's goal settled the issue for Stoke.

However, Tony Waddington, who was at the helm in 1972, had travelled down on a supporters' coach from Clayton. After the game he approached the Radio Stoke team wondering how he was going to make his way back, because the supporters' coach had departed. I was surprised that he hadn't been invited to the club's celebratory banquet in the evening.

However, he hopped into our Radio Stoke car and as we passed the convoy of coaches going home via the M1 , Tony wound his window down and waved to them all... they enjoyed waving back.

Ten years later I was back at Wembley for the Autowindscreens Trophy Final against Bristol City with Gudjon Thordarson, the Icelander, in charge at the end of his first season. Graham Kavanagh and Peter Thorne secured the trophy for the Potters with two outstanding goals. This time the commentary position was along the edge of the stand roof above the Royal Box. A superb view, but not ideal for anyone suffering from vertigo.

Cocky Cardiff at Ninian Park in the play-off semi-final second leg in 2002 was a real commentary cracker. The Bluebirds were super confident that they would seal a victory having won the first leg at the Britannia Stadium 2-1. In fact with time ebbing away and the game goalless, the PA announcer asked the Cardiff fans not to celebrate on the pitch. That must have galvanised the Potters.

In the final moments of normal time James O'Connor scored to level matters and send the game into extra time. It was O'Connor again whose shot hit substitute Souleymane Oulare's backside and flew into the net five minutes from the end of extra time. The Potters were on their way to the Millennium Stadium to take on Brentford in the play-off final.

May 11th, 2002 and a superb commentary position at the Millennium Stadium opposite the tunnel. 42,000 were in place, the majority Stoke City fans, as Deon Burton struck for the Potters just after the quarter hour. On the stroke of half-time a shot from Bjarni Gudjonsson was deflected into the Brentford net by Ben Burgess and that was it. Tremendous celebrations at the end and promotion for the Potters to the First Division (now, of course, the Championship).

But no one knew at the time that the Icelandic Consortium were about to sack the manager they had put in place, Gudjon Thordarson. He had delivered promotion; they delivered the bullet.

I've had some wonderful moments as both a spectator and a commentator following Stoke City. I hope that you enjoy the great games that follow in this most interesting book.

Nigel Johnson
BBC Radio Stoke commentator
chairman, Sir Stanley Matthews Foundation

DENNIS HEROD: BORN 27 OCTOBER 1923, TUNSTALL; 340 GAMES, 1 GOAL

Dennis Herod

Sheffield United 2 Stoke City 1

League Division One

Saturday 14 June 1947

IT'S EVER SO simple why I have chosen the match of my life. It's because it was probably the most important moment of my life. It may seem strange that I have chosen a game that Stoke didn't win, but this match meant everything. Everything.

I was born and bred in Stoke and I lived just down from the Victoria Ground and I love Stoke City and to have a chance to win the League Championship, or the Premiership as they call it now, was incredible. We were one match away, just one win, and we would have won it for my hometown club. Nobody could pick a bigger occasion and I would chose that against any game when I personally had a great match or even the game at Aston Villa when I got injured and managed to score a goal while being a passenger on the wing. That's a match I remember certainly, but it still doesn't compare to the day we should have won the title.

THE 1946/47 SEASON was an incredible time to be a professional footballer. The war was only just over, the country was in the grip of rationing, National Service kept men away from their homes, food and clothing were scarce and despite the fact that the war had ended, there was little to latch on to if you were the average working man. What they did grab a hold of was football. The crowds were terrific. Thousands upon thousands would come to see us and Stoke actually had an average gate of above 30,000 for the only time in their history. To be a footballer then felt like the birds were singing all day and the sun shone. It was fantastic.

Part of the reason was because everyone felt released from the terribly onerous problems which war had brought. They weren't over at all as I've said, but mothers and fathers weren't living in the terrible expectation of receiving a letter or telegram telling them that their son had died in the line of duty. Husbands were returning home to be reunited with the wives they hadn't seen in years and sport was the common bond which brought everyone together. People went mad for football.

I WAS LUCKY to be alive. I had seen active service in North Africa and Italy in the 44th Tank regiment. I wasn't a blood thirsty type. I didn't want to be in C Squadron 5 troop. I didn't want to be in the tank crew and I didn't want to be there when my tank was hit by enemy fire and two of my buddies were killed. I was doing my duty, but every night I would say to myself, 'Dennis, these are your last days.' It was a fatalistic approach that many of us had. We had a job to do, but I didn't want to kill anybody and I didn't want to be killed. It was a pretty dreadful existence.

We got to France on D-Day itself and it was our job to patrol the perimeter of our lines at night to ensure there was no counter-attack while the rest of the army slept. We'd stand to at dusk and then stand down again an hour before dawn. By this time we were near Caen, where the Germans were holding out tooth and nail. This one night the Allies sent in a thousand bomber raid which was designed to sort the garrison out there. I remember looking up and seeing the sky was black with planes.

I got wounded on 7th August 1944. I was very lucky because two of my crew were killed when the shell hit us. I was knocked unconscious, but only had a fractured jaw although I lost most of my teeth. I was then even luckier, though, because my war was over and I was taken to Manchester to be treated. After they'd patched me up there, I was transferred to Trentham Park to convalesce. Well, that was great. Where do you think I would rather be – Trentham Park or Caen?

Once I was fit enough I began playing for Stoke again in October 1944. The manager Bob McGrory used to invite the camp commander Captain Bedford down to the ground and he had a seat in the Stoke boardroom for games. In fact we had a camp team at Trentham Park and we entered the Staffordshire Junior Cup and I think if we'd won it, the captain would have kept me there to defend the title! Eventually I was released from the camp and could go home and enjoy life again.

LEAGUE FOOTBALL DIDN'T start straight after the war, because of travel restrictions. The first season, 1945/46, they split the clubs from the top two divisions north and south. The matches were still quite competitive. I remember one game at Newcastle, who were actually in the Second Division at the time. They had a centre-forward called Albert Stubbins and before the game I was told he couldn't head the ball anymore. Needless to say by half-time it was 3-1 to Newcastle and Stubbins had scored a hat-trick of headers. He eventually scored five goals in a 9-1 win that I prefer to forget, although I do remember that I got the Man of the Match in *The People* newspaper match report!

The other match that sticks in my mind from that season was the FA Cup quarter-final against Bolton. The FA Cup was run that season as it was possible to play those one off games and that match attracted a phenomenal crowd to Burnden Park of over 65,000. There was a tremendous crush and just after we kicked off I had people spilling on to the pitch around my goal. That wasn't so unusual in those days because of the huge crowds that saw every game. I was concentrating on the game of course, but I soon realised that there was some problem and I asked a policeman what was going on. He told me that some of the people had fainted. Then I looked at them properly, and remember I had been in Africa and France and I had seen plenty of dead bodies, and I knew those people hadn't fainted. I knew those people were dead.

Altogether 33 people died that day. The authorities made us play on though and we lost 2-0. But I will never be able to get those images out of my head.

WE HAD A great side, including some wonderfully talented players. Of course on the right wing was Stanley Matthews, who was incomparable as far as I was concerned. He was already a living legend, despite the fact he was only 32, but of course that meant he was in theory coming to the end of his career. He could beat any full-back and leave him for dead over the first few yards. I remember one match against Manchester United just after the war when he tied their full-back Billy McGlen in knots to the point that the crowd were in fits of laughter at McGlen's efforts to keep Stan under some sort of control.

Stan set a record for becoming the most capped English international just after the war too. He earned his 44th cap to break Arsenal skipper Eddie Hapgood's record. He should have won many more if you ask me, but the fool selectors didn't always keep faith with a man whose mercurial talent was on a different level to mere mortals.

Then we had a star centre-forward called Freddie Steele. Personally I would put him amongst the world's greats. As far as I was concerned he was the most complete footballer I have ever seen in my life. He could do everything. He could head so powerfully, he was nicknamed 'Nobby' by the fans because he was so good with his nob, or head. He used to train by jumping to head a ball tied to a string under the old wooden stand at the Vic. He could hit the ball cleanly with both feet and he could hit it hard too. I was glad I didn't have to face him except in training – and that was difficult enough! He was Stoke's highest ever scorer for a long time until John Ritchie came along and broke his record. But Freddie had scored another 90 goals or so during wartime matches, which are not counted among official statistics, so he really scored about 75 goals more for Stoke than anyone else. He was an incredible goalscorer.

Neil Franklin was the best centre-half I ever saw. He was so confident on the ball. I remember he used to cause me all sorts of problems because you never knew what he was going to do next. If a long ball was played over the top he'd shout to me, "Dennis, come on. It's yours." And I'd race out to come and collect the ball only to find that he'd turn on it and waltz away up the field with both myself and the forward, who had heard him shout, expecting a backpass. I remember Bob McGrory used to get hot under the collar because Neil would dribble his way out of trouble rather than clear his lines by putting his boot through the ball. Neil would trap the ball in the six-yard box and take on a couple of players before finding a pass for a team-mate and McGrory would be in the dugout shouting and screaming for him to kick it into the stand!

Neil had such class and such quality in both feet. He was selected for England for the first time in the 1946/47 season to replace the retired England captain Stan Cullis at centre-half. He was actually never dropped by England and set a then record of 27 consecutive games for his country. That was an incredible record as the selectors would rarely keep faith with a player for more than a few games as Stan Matthews found out to his cost. It was only when Neil got fed up with the way footballers were treated and paid in 1950 and decided to take up an offer to play in Bogota, Colombia that he lost his place. They were not affiliated to FIFA at the time and so that disqualified Neil from playing for England. And he had broken his contract with Stoke too, so they transferred him to Hull when he came back from Colombia after only a few months because he didn't like the change in lifestyle. It was a very sad end for such a wonderful player. I often think that Billy Wright, who took over from Neil as England's centre-half, would not have been the first player to win a century of caps for England if Neil had kept playing. It would have been Neil.

There were plenty of other good players in our team such as the full-backs John McCue and Billy Mould, half-backs Frank Mountford and Johnny Sellars and the left wing pairing of Frank Baker and Alec Ormston, who were rated by many as the best left wing partnership in the country.

Bob McGrory, the manager, had played a record number of games for the club as a right-back. He was a gruff, terse Scot, who liked a tot or two of whisky, but didn't stand any nonsense from the players. He unearthed some great talents which he brought together as a team. Throughout the war he had kept the club playing football while many other sides did not always play because all their players had gone to war. Aston Villa, for example, rarely played at the start of the war. But McGrory reasoned that when the war ended he would need players that had experience and he was proved right in that. A lot of us who were youngsters in 1939 when war broke out such as myself, John McCue, Billy Mould and Neil Franklin were first team regulars by the time it ended. They called us the '£10 team' because we'd only cost the club our £10 signing-on fees.

One of the greatest things about that team was the fact that often we were able to field an eleven of great players who all came from Stoke-on-Trent. There has always been a lot of talent around the area, but at that time we had a whole squad. In fact, of our regular first team, only our captain Jock Kirton was not a local lad. He was a tough Scots left-half, who was a very underrated player. The other player not to come from the area was George Mountford, who hailed from Kidderminster. He was Stan Matthews' understudy on the right wing.

I always thought that I was the weak link in the side. I was a good goalkeeper. I was brave and would dive at forwards' feet when they came through and got knocked out several times for my pains! I could punch too. But I never felt I was quite as good as the side deserved. Maybe that shows a bit of a lack of self-confidence, but it was how I felt. The one player we did miss that season was inside-forward Frank Bowyer. He was only a youngster like me, but he'd got plenty of experience during the war and had scored a lot goals. He had the most tremendous volley in his right foot, but unfortunately for us Frank was not available for the whole season due to being on duty abroad in the Armed Forces. We missed him and the inside-right position caused us a lot of problems with inconsistent performances from his various replacements throughout the season.

THE WINTER OF 1947 was an unbelievable. It actually followed a very hot summer, which had led to water shortages, but the amount of rain that fell on the opening day of the season seemed to make up for that! We drew 2-2 with Charlton to get our campaign underway, and after that we had little idea that it would end up with us in with a chance of the league title. In fact we lost the next three games, but then won six in a row to put us up there with the leaders.

The weather caused multiple postponements and because there were restrictions on playing sporting events on any day other than a Saturday because the government wanted people to concentrate on working during the week, the rearranged matches could only take place after the end of the season, meaning a total revamp of the fixture list. It would now go on until the middle of June.

After Christmas our season went very well. We had a run when we went 16 games and only lost one match. Right at the end of the season, when it was all coming to a head, we won seven on the trot. We had a fantastic Easter winning the three games we played on Good Friday, Easter Saturday and Easter Monday, scoring 11 goals and only conceding two.

I had just got back into the team then after losing my place initially because of injury. I'd ended up with concussion in an incredible game at Middlesbrough when we lost 5-4 to a last minute goal. Their centre-forward Andy Donaldson shoulder-charged me into the back of the net, but all the referee said was, "He barely touched you." I could feel a large lump growing on my forehead and so pointed it out to the referee saying, "Where did this come from then?" It didn't make any difference. He still allowed the goal that was scored.

I spent the next week after that in bed recovering and then contracted flu, so McGrory brought in Arthur Jepson from Port Vale for £3,750 to play in goal. He did very well and so I couldn't displace him until Stoke lost a two-goal lead to draw at Everton in March. Jepson got the blame for that result and in fact only played for Stoke once after that.

Arthur was a nice fellow who actually was a county cricketer as well. He bowled for Nottinghamshire alongside Harold Larwood, the great England bowler and later became a Test match umpire.

Our seven match-winning run put us right up there in contention – not least because when the fixtures were redrawn, we ended up with a couple of games in hand. So we always felt we were in with a chance. That form put us right in contention for the title. There were four sides left in it – Liverpool, Manchester United, Wolves and ourselves - and with three games to go we all stood a chance.

IF YOU HAD to win three matches to win the league title would you sell the best player in the world? Well, that's what Bob McGrory did.

It was madness, and the result of a jealousy which had grown over a decade; emanating from an incident before the war when Stan had asked for a transfer because he was fed up with the way he was being treated. It had led to protests among supporters and eventually, after much to-ing and fro-ing and reams of newspaper headlines, he had agreed to stay. But it hadn't been forgotten all these years later as there had been renewed problems between Stan and McGrory all season. McGrory thought that because Stan now lived in Blackpool he wanted to pick and choose the games he played in and that he also wouldn't play through minor injuries for the team. I remember overhearing them having a bawling argument in the tunnel after training one day. Well, all season these disputes went on. First Stan said he was injured so wouldn't play against Chelsea, but then he declared himself fit for the following Saturday to play at Arsenal. McGrory didn't take to Stan assuming he'd be selected in the side as without him they had produced a superb result to win 5-2 at Chelsea. So McGrory asked Matthews to play in the reserves and Stan refused.

After that got resolved following a couple of weeks' stand-off Stan refused to play at Grimsby on Good Friday on the basis that the hotel he ran in Blackpool had taken a glut of bookings and so he wouldn't be able to make it across to Blundell Park, but could make it to Stoke the next day to play in the return game. As you can imagine that didn't go down well with the manager.

It wasn't a problem for me, because you have to trust people like Stan. He knew when he could and couldn't play. But the whole situation did cause a lot of heartache. There were more newspaper headlines, a fans' meeting at the King's Hall, and the whole thing got out of hand.

McGrory really did not like the fact that Stan lived in Blackpool and trained up there. He effectively only came down to Stoke for matches, and when he was injured we didn't see him at all, so McGrory couldn't keep tabs on him. He also hated Stan's popularity with supporters. He didn't particularly like Neil Franklin for the same reason either. The player McGrory loved was Freddie Steele, who kept quiet, got on with things and did what his manager told him.

So McGrory agreed to sell Stan to Blackpool for £11,500 with three games left of the season. It was an obvious move because Stan had guested for Blackpool throughout the war as he had been stationed nearby as a PT instructor in the RAF. He now owned his hotel there and had a family. He didn't want to move back into the smoke and grime of the post-war Potteries. You could argue that it was a good deal as the transfer record at the time was £14,000 and Stan was 32. But the effect it had on our morale was devastating. We had sold the world's best player and it didn't go down very well with either fans or players no matter what spin McGrory tried to put on it.

McGrory could be so callous sometimes. They used to announce the teams about five minutes before the kick-off at the Victoria Ground and Stan would always have been announced to be in the side in the paper the night before to ensure that he put three or four thousand on the gate. But then at five to three they'd announce the actual teams and when it got to No. 7 and it was this lad called Syd Peppitt, the crowd used to boo. They wanted Matthews, that's why they'd come. We could hear the boos in the dressing room. You could hear them at Mow Cop.

Syd was a real lovely person and my heart used to bleed for him. It was criminal what McGrory did to him, using him like that. And then he expected him to go out and face that lot, who didn't want him and put in a decent performance? How stupid. Peppit had been an England youth international so he had plenty of talent, but he was ripped apart by that. Talk about destroying a man morally.

WE DREW 0-0 with Sunderland in our last match at home. It was a frustrating afternoon and performance, which seemed to have put us out of it, but then in our penultimate match we won at Villa Park, 1-0 thanks to a George Mountford goal. Manchester United had now finished their season and were only a point ahead of us on 56 points. Wolves and Liverpool still had one game remaining, but it was against each other and so would be something of a title decider at Molineux on 7 June as whichever side won would be top of the league. In fact if Wolves won they would clinch the title as they would have 58 points and we only had one game left and would not be able to catch them as we were on 55. But if Liverpool won, they'd be top, but only two points ahead of us; and we had a better goal difference. Liverpool won 2-1, thanks to a goal from my old nemesis Albert Stubbins, who had moved to Liverpool at the start of the season, and that left us in with a chance. Liverpool had only 57 points. We had to go to Sheffield United and win our last game. The scoreline didn't matter. We just had to win.

THAT WAS WHEN things really started to go wrong. We were taken on a trip to Ireland, which was supposed to keep us occupied, while we waited the two weeks until that last game, because Sheffield still had one more league match to play on the intervening Saturday, but it turned into an absolute disaster. I think Neil started it off. We got to Holyhead to catch the ferry and he'd forgotten his passport. Well, we were going to Southern Ireland, so he needed it, and it caused a bit of consternation and we had to wait for the next ferry while they phoned back to his house and got someone to bring his passport out. It was incredibly cold while we waited as well; a bitter, frosty night in late May!

It was hardly deluxe travelling either. We were now on the overnight ferry and the directors had only paid for us to travel 'steerage' – the lowest class of travel. A storm broke late that night; a deluge like you've never seen. The crossing was rough, so rough in fact that several of the team were heavily sick and didn't recover for a couple of days after we'd arrived in Ireland.

It didn't get any better when we got there. We played a benefit match up at Linfield first and we got to the ground only to discover that Neil had forgotten his boots! Then the following evening we played another game at Drumcondra in Dublin and in that match Alec Ormston pulled a ligament. As I say, that was a disastrous tour. We were delighted to get home.

PEOPLE REACT SO differently to stress. Any normal Saturday morning was a dreadful time for me. I had a few cigarettes while I worried about having a bad day, etc, etc, etc. it used to affect me so badly. I was focussing on what I had to do and it got to me.

In the olden days at Stoke City, there was only one toilet in the home dressing room in the stand and you couldn't get in there before kick-off because Stan Matthews was in there being sick, as he used to before every game. And if it wasn't him then Freddie Steele would be in there – and he was even worse. Remember these were top, top players who had played for England in front of 149,000 at Hampden Park.

I roomed on away trips with Freddie Steele. He was the scruffiest man alive. He still had his army vest, which he wore constantly during the day and even to sleep in, even though he'd been demobbed a year or so. I would wake up at three or four o'clock in the morning to discover him pacing round the room, worried and smoking another cigarette.

But then there was Neil Franklin who would be outside at ten to three talking to people, chatting and not worried in the slightest. He'd then pop into the dressing room get changed and trot out to play! Neil was an incredibly calm character, but don't let that fool you into thinking he didn't care. He cared with a passion. He just had this cavalier air about him.

So you can imagine how I was feeling on the morning of the Sheffield United game. This was it; the biggest game of my life and the biggest game in Stoke City's history.

SHEFFIELD UNITED WERE our bogey side really. They had knocked us out of the FA Cup that season with a fluke goal when a cross in the last minute dropped over goalkeeper Jepson into the net to secure them a 1-0 victory. They had won the League North title in 1945/46 and were guaranteed to finish sixth this season whatever the result. They'd been in wretched form in the run up to the game having been thrashed 6-2 at Manchester United.

I am also sure that Liverpool offered Sheffield a bonus for beating us. When we got to the ground, Sheffield had locked themselves into their own dressing room which was very unusual, so I was sure something was going on.

There were thousands of Stoke fans there who had travelled across the Pennines in the hope of seeing the team win the first serious trophy in its history. They gave us tremendous support with a chorus of rattles.

The match didn't start very well to say the least. In fact it started in a dreadful manner. After just a couple of minutes Sheffield scored. One of their best players, Jimmy Hagan, their England international inside-forward, who I thought was a great player anyway, had gone on holiday and this old forward called Jack Pickering played instead. He was 38 and hadn't played in their first team all season. And of course he is the one who scores. Pickering didn't even hit his shot very well. We'd left him unmarked about eight yards out, but even then he didn't hit it properly. Nine times out of ten I would have stopped that shot. But this time I didn't. I dived over it as it bobbled towards me. The defence had left him unmarked, but I still blame myself for not saving the ball. I should have done and then maybe things would have been different. Maybe then you'd be sitting here reading a chapter about a glorious victory, but instead the ball went in and we were behind so very early on. It's given me nightmares ever since.

So they were winning 1-0, but straight away Alec Ormston equalised. Freddie Steele put George Mountford away down the right hand side and he crossed for Steele to get on the end of it and head it down for Alec to shoot home from close range. We were on top then and had what looked like a cast-iron penalty appeal turned down by the referee when Steele was tripped by Latham. I think he gave United the benefit of the doubt because of the pitch conditions. I remember I made one really good save that day, from their centre-forward Collindridge, who headed from close range, but I managed to tip it round the post and we went into the break tied at 1-1.

After half-time we were encamped in their half of the field trying to find that vital, vital breakthrough. We had all the play, but again we let them break away. As they did so, John McCue had a tackle he had to make, but he missed it because he slipped over in the mud. So Sheffield broke down field unchecked towards me and Walter Rickett scored their second goal. Try as we might we could not score. The pitch was horrendous and didn't help, but we got increasingly desperate with our attacks. I ended up with not a lot to do for the remainder of the game, so all I could do was watch as chance after chance slipped past. Their goalkeeper, Smith, tipped George Mountford's shot on to the bar and then a goalmouth scramble saw the ball run loose, but Peppitt and Mountford got in each other's way when I thought one of them had to score.

The weather, in keeping with how it had been all season, was atrocious. It had rained all week and it rained again the night before the game making the pitch incredibly heavy, with plenty of pools of water lying on the surface. Remember it was the middle of June! It really wasn't in any condition for the importance of the match we were playing. But we had to get on with it, although I still maintain that the pitch played a massive part in us failing to win.

Another factor was the fact that in those days Bramall Lane was also used for playing cricket and one side of the pitch did not have a stand running alongside it. There was a huge gap where the cricket square and the remainder of the outfield was and all Sheffield had to do was knock the ball as far as they could down there and it would take ages to get it back. Time and again they kicked it over there with the whole of the cricket field to aim at. How many minutes was the ball out of play? Bloody loads I can tell you. That cost us too.

Of course there was no multi-ball system in operation back then. Aside from the fact that it hadn't been thought of, we just didn't have enough balls anyway. This was post-war Britain. We were lucky to have a new ball at all to play the matches with. Often it wasn't, it would be a ball that had been used a few times before.

AS THE HALF wore on, the mud sapped the strength from the boys' legs and our attacks grew less and less frenzied. Eventually we could run no more and the game ended tamely. They beat us 2-1 and when the final whistle went I was devastated. I can't tell you how depressing it was. The atmosphere was dreadful. It took me months to be able to smile again. It still hurts me now, talking about it. I felt guilty. Luckily a draw wouldn't have made a blind bit of difference, so the fact I helped give them a 1-0 start hadn't totally cost us, but it was so early in the game that I can't help feel I was at fault. So how did I feel? How do you think? We'd come so, so close.

I think I was the luckiest person in the world. For 15 years, to do something that you love to do and gives you the greatest pleasure and to get paid for being with real nice people and be the focus of the working man's hopes and dreams. The game was so good to me. I'm getting a bit sentimental now, but what a lucky person I was.

JOHNNY KING: BORN 9 AUGUST 1932, WRENBURY; 311 GAMES, 114 GOALS

Johnny King

Nottingham Forest 0 Stoke City 3

League Division Two

Wednesday 25 August 1954

IT'S A LONG way back to my era – mid-seventies, mid-70s; that's my age now, not seventies the decade! I played longer ago than that! 1953 I kicked off at Stoke – only over 50 years ago!

Stoke came in for me that September. We'd had a good side at Crewe. Winger Frank Blunstone had been sold to Chelsea, where he would eventually win the League title in 1954/55. My move came out of the blue for me. I didn't have an inkling of what was going on. I hadn't long come out of the army actually. March 15th 1953 I was demobbed. I remember the date. During my National Service I'd been able to keep playing football. I was only a clerk in REME (Royal Electrical and Mechanical Engineers), which meant I'd still been able to appear for Crewe regularly as I was stationed at Ellesmere in Shropshire. At that time I earned £1 8s a week in the army, but £6 a match for Crewe. So I was a rich man on that army base. If I played twice a week I had £12 in my pocket.

I'd scored quite a few goals for Crewe, which is what attracted Frank Taylor's notice. He'd only been Stoke manager for a year following relegation from the First Division in 1953 under retiring manager Bob McGrory. So I signed and had a great few years at the club. I actually I didn't really get on with Frank Taylor. He was a gent, but you knew that Tony Waddington would progress. He'd started as a part-time trainer at around the time I joined, in fact I think he was instrumental in getting me signed as he knew what was going on over in Crewe, living that way. Waddo went from part-time reserve coach, to A team coach, to assistant coach of the first team and in charge of the reserves, to first team coach and you just knew he would take over eventually. But Taylor was quite aloof, whereas Waddo would always look after you, giving you a few match tickets and the like to make you feel good.

When I was first playing in the first team we hadn't got cars or anything like that. We had to use the bus and train. If we'd had a good game we'd be there on the bus proud as punch making sure everyone could see us, but if you'd had a bad game you'd turn your collars up and hide and you'd listen to all the supporters saying, "That King, wasn't he a load of crap"!

WE HAD SOME good players at Stoke during my time. Inside-forward Frank Bowyer was a fantastic player. He'd been around for ages and was the playmaker of the side. He was great with us new boys too. He got Don Ratcliffe his first game actually. Taylor asked Frank who he wanted play outside him at right wing and he said that he wanted Ratter. He told Don, "When I get the ball, you run." In fact he made Don look good, as he'd be delivering these 40 or 50 yard passes to him on the wing, but Don was already on the move, while the full-back could only react to the pass, and so Don collected the ball with a four or five yard headstart.

Being experienced, Bowyer used to keep his eye on you as you bedded in. I remember he also gave Don a lesson in how to play the game in a training match when he was a real youngster. Don was having a nightmare, always turning into trouble, playing with his head down and this one time Bowyer passed the ball to Don and he did it again and lost the ball. Frank came over to him and said, "Hey, you're supposed to know what you're going to do with the ball before you get it." And he was right. It gave me pause for thought that too. It helped Don no end because he kept his head up then and looked around as the ball came to him and he was ready to use it, rather than waiting to control it and then wondering what would be on. It was like a light bulb going on, and he helped all of us like that.

Frank was also an expert volleyer. He had a hell of a shot in his right foot. He had huge thighs and he generated a lot of speed when he whipped his leg through to hit a ball. He was a lovely guy as well.

He had lots of interests outside football. He had a newsagents in Shelton and he bought two hairdressers shops for his daughters. Believe it or not he also used to keep pigs!

Another experienced player was Frank Mountford. He was an unbelievable player, so committed. He threw himself into every tackle and had a great engine. His trademark was a sliding tackle which would leave him covered from head to foot in mud. He had converted from wing-half to centre-half when Neil Franklin went off to Bogota and got himself suspended from playing football and eventually transferred to Hull.

Frank lived life a bit. He liked a drink and a smoke. When he finished in the late 1950s, Frank got a job as trainer, but there was no job for Frank Bowyer when he retired. He'd lived the life of a saint. It's ironic isn't it?

ANOTHER HARD MAN was our left-back John McCue. He was the original 'Chopper' – not that Ron Harris. Not many got past him, and if they did, they didn't do it again! His attitude was 'none shall pass'. I thought he was a good player. A sheer stopper. He was one who wasn't a full-time professional. That was possible in those days. He worked as a PT instructor at one of the pits, keeping miners fit and exercised. He was in his mid-thirties by then as he'd played in the side that so nearly won the league in 1947 like Mountford. John used to always be moaning about how the directors of the club were threatening us in order to keep our wages down.

Then the other full-back on the right hand side was George Bourne. He was a lovely fellow. He broke his leg against Manchester United. It was a bad break and finished him.

Right-winger Johnny Malkin also got crocked. His cruciate ligament went in his knee. He got fit again, but without the ligament, he couldn't turn. He was great in a straight line, but couldn't play again because he couldn't turn.

Half-back Johnny Sellars was another one who was a part-timer. The best way to describe Johnny is to say that he didn't wash with our soap! He was a classy gentleman. He wouldn't come in the bath with us and use the floating soap that all the lads used to use, he'd bring his own soap in and go in the showers, but he was all right. He'd been part of the team the that nearly won the title in 1947 as well.

After McCue finished, his replacement at left-back was Tony 'Tadger' Allen. He was a top bloke. A good footballer, bloody brilliant in fact. He got capped by England at a very young age.

In goal we had Bill Robertson, who was a good keeper and a gentleman. His positioning was fantastic. He wasn't a spectacular diver because he didn't often need to dive, his positioning was so good. He had terrible teeth because he was terrified of the dentist. His fear was that bad he used to fill his teeth with chewing gum!

Then there was left-winger Harry Oscroft. He packed a hell of a shot into his left foot. It was nearly as good as mine! He used to cut inside, but then cut back on to his left foot and whack it. He tended to blast his shots, whereas I could hammer them, or chip or beat the keeper one on one. Stoke exchanged him for Dicky Cunliffe from Port Vale, who was a player that didn't make the step up to First Division football. Harry scored over 100 goals for Stoke, same as me.

Centre-forward Andy Graver came to Stoke from Lincoln for £11,000. He could actually hang in the air. He seemed as if he was hanging anyway. He was a good header of the ball and a real character. Andy didn't really make it at Second Division level, though.

The forward who was a success at Stoke was my partner-in-crime George Kelly. He was a great little inside-forward who used to score about 20 goals a year, but all of them were from about three feet. He was the goal poacher supreme. We vied to be top scorer for most of the 1950s, although sometimes Harry Oscroft beat us to it!

Ken Thomson was our captain. He was the centre-half and a great stopper. He was a gruff Scotsman, who loved golf. In fact he died of a heart attack on a golf course at a very young age only just after he'd finished playing. But he was a rock in our defence. He was a good captain too. He didn't stand any nonsense and made sure you all pulled your weight.

I USED TO love playing against big centre-halves myself. I used to murder Jackie Charlton at Leeds. I remember him once getting so frustrated with not being able to get a hold of me that he started moaning to the referee – he loved a moan did Jackie – and he started up, "Referee! He's getting under me!" and then I turned around and there was Big Jack Charlton – The Giraffe as he was known – moaning his head off! I had some blinders against him and I quite liked playing Big John Charles too – in fact any big centre-half struggled to cope with me.

I was good on the deck, but I couldn't head a ball to save my life. I was all one foot – very left-footed, although I always think that left-footers stand out, because so many players are right-footed, so you notice the left-footed ones more. I used to turn centre-halves, back into them and draw a foul with the referee thinking they were trying to climb over me. I could also trap the ball under pressure. I was quick and I loved to spread the play by bending the ball with the outside of my left foot for either winger to run on to. I spent my whole youth practising with a tennis ball as the school I went to was too poor to have proper footballs. I practised against a wall and learnt to hit a ball with power and to bend it with the outside of my foot. You don't see that so much these days. Players love to bend it with the inside of the foot, but not the outside.

I GOT FIVE hat-tricks in my Stoke career and one big head! My favourite was the hat-trick I scored at Nottingham Forest in 1954/55, one of the seasons we should have gone up. My other hat-tricks came against Swansea in a 5-0 win in my first season, 1953/54, and then I scored a hat-trick on Christmas Day 1954, against Bury in a 3-2 win. The following season I bagged three at Doncaster on the opening day of the season in a 4-2 win, but probably the most memorable came in my final season, 1960/61, in the incredible 9-0 victory over Plymouth. Stoke were having a terrible time at that point. Waddo had only just been made manager, and he'd yet to transform the club. We were struggling and I'd only scored three goals in 20 games up to that point. Crowds were way down and in fact only 6,500 or so turned up to watch that game the weekend before Christmas. But somehow it all come together that day and everything we hit flew in. I always like to think that is Stoke's biggest ever victory, although for some reason the record books give a 10-3 win over West Brom before the War. That's ridiculous if you ask me. We won by nine goals – nine goals! They may have scored ten against West Brom, but they let three in – that's only a seven-goal winning margin. Someone should rewrite the record books!

At the start of 1954/55 Frank Bowyer was absent for two months because of being hospitalised by a stomach complaint, so we were actually missing arguably our best and most creative player, but the season got underway fantastically well with five wins in the first six games. We beat Birmingham on the opening Saturday 2-1 thanks to goals from Joey Hutton, deputising for Frank, and Harry Oscroft.

I remember that game was played in a torrential downpour, typical Potteries weather for mid-August! Birmingham took the lead through Warhurst just after half-time, but Hutton belted in a terrific shot into the roof of the net from distance to equalise straight away and Oscroft scored the winner from close range ten minutes from time. But I'll never forget that rain, my word. We were splashing around in puddles for most of the second half. I think Harry's winning goal came because the ball, for once, didn't stick as it came across from the right and it carried through to him on the left hand side of the box and he put it past Gil Merrick in the Birmingham goal.

Full-back John Short came into the team that season. He was the only new signing, arriving from Wolves. Joey Hutton and Bobby Cairns had arrived from Ayr United the previous Christmas, just after me. They were great mates. They came as a package. Cairns was a good player. Not the strongest in the tackle, but good going forward. They hadn't really broken into the side at that stage, but Cairns became a regular for four or five seasons after that, moving back to play at wing-half after starting out as an inside-forward. Hutton played that season until Bowyer was ready again, but after that he faded out of the picture. With them and me up front, we had a very small forward line. No one more than 5ft 9in tall! Hardly Nat Lofthouse!!

FOREST HAD LOST their opening match 3-0 at Luton, so we felt confident of a result. Mind you, they'd only just missed out on promotion the previous season. Apparently Stoke hadn't won at Forest since 1928/29, so there were plenty of omens against us.

We played really well, though. Our passing was great, and we dominated a much more physical side by keeping possession and trying to work openings. Having a small forward line could work both ways, but on this occasion we did run rings round Forest a bit. My first goal came from a Johnny Malkin cross, which I finished off left-footed.

We didn't have goal celebrations then. We just used to shake hands and jog back to the halfway line... Job done.

We made bundles more chances, but I missed a few, to be honest, and I should have scored more, but then we were handed a chance to put the game safe when I was hauled down by their right-back Ware as I was in on goal. These days it would have been deemed a professional foul and he would have been off, but I was just happy with the chance to score a second goal – and I did.

Penalties were my speciality. I loved them. I always took them the same – outside of the left foot to the goalkeeper's right. That was my way. I hit them with power and always in the same place. It was difficult for keepers to do the research they do these days, because no games were on TV, so you could do the same thing over and over again as they wouldn't know.

The second pen came from a handball, again by Ware – he didn't have a good night, bless him! We were comfortable after that and it took until injury time for Forest to muster a shot on target. I remember their supporters gave an ironical cheer when Bill Robertson was finally forced to make a save.

In fact the only real chance Forest had came form a bit of a mix up in our defence, not from their own play. A long ball was punted to the edge of our area and Ken Thomson and Bill Robertson got in a bit of a muddle between them. I think either both of them called for it, or neither of them. Anyway, Ken, being a good stopper centre-half, opted to try to clear the ball back upfield, but only succeeded in smashing it against Frank Mountford, who was also covering back! Not a Forest player in sight, three Stoke players and the ball ricochets off Frank and dribbles slowly towards the goal as all three collapse in a heap! Thankfully it went inches past the post. But it tells you something about how dominant we were that that was Forest's best chance!

IT WAS 7.30PM kick-offs in those days because floodlights were a rarity and we had to get the game over before the light went. And it was only a ten minute interval at half-time, not quarter of an hour. So the game was over by ten past nine. At the time I was still living at Nantwich, so it was straight into the bath for five minutes and off. The Stoke chairman, Charlie Salmon, who made his money as a newsagent in the Potteries, gave me a lift back to Stoke station, where I caught the five past eleven train back to Crewe and then a taxi back home. They wouldn't pay to put me up for the night in the Potteries, oh no! They had to get me home! So that was my celebration. Scored a hat-trick and then straight back home! It was all glamour in them days wasn't it!

We won six out of the first seven games that season, so we had a great start. We continued by beating Middlesbrough 2-1 at their place to record Stoke's first ever victory at Ayresome Park, but then things tailed off. In fact it all went pear-shaped. We only won three games between 11th December and 28th March. That's not promotion form. One other memorable game came when we won 4-2 at Liverpool – we used to win a few times there, in fact I played in the last Stoke team ever to win there. We won 4-3 in 1959 and I think Stoke have only drawn there a couple of times since!

Although I scored two hat-tricks and 20 goals in all that season, I didn't finish as the club's leading scorer. That honour fell to left winger Harry Oscroft. He scored 21 times.

We weren't a great side during the 50s if I'm honest. Good, solid, but not quite good enough to go up. We had a couple of goes at promotion while I was at the club, one of them in that season, 1954/55, when we came within two points of going up. We'd let things slip from our good start that season, so on the last day there were five sides in with a chance of filling one of the top two places (only two clubs were promoted from each division at that time). We were fourth, so we travelled to Plymouth for our last game knowing that if we won and two of the other sides didn't, we'd be up. But we didn't play that well and Plymouth needed the win to avoid relegation, and they beat us 2-0. That promotion push was not helped either by Bobby Cairns being called up for National Service and being absent for several weeks doing his training for the Forces.

Another of the reasons we didn't keep our run going was our epic third round FA Cup tie with Bury which has gone down in history. That match was in the Guinness Book of Records for the longest ever FA Cup tie. It went to five matches, we just couldn't be separated. It was ridiculous really. It even went into extra time in the fifth match. We were all fed up with playing in this game, so with the scores tied at 2-2 a cross came into the penalty area. There was a bit of a scrum, which ended up with Don Ratcliffe falling on top of the Bury goalkeeper. But Don didn't get up, he stayed lying on the keeper, who by now was making a tremendous racket! The ball came back into the box and Tim Coleman slid over in the mud, the ball hit him on the head, flew up into the air and into the far corner. The keeper went mad at the referee, but he still gave the goal and we were through!

The five games knackered us though as they had to be crammed into the schedule and we went out in the next round at Swansea, but it cost us some league points too as we were very tired indeed!

We also nearly got promotion in 1956/57 when we were well in contention around the end of February when we beat Lincoln 8-0. Our right-winger Tim Coleman scored seven goals that day, but everyone forgets that I scored the other goal! We then drew 1-1 at Sheffield United who were in the mix for promotion as well and we thought we were really on for something. We were ??th with 43 points after 33 games.

But then it all fell apart. We lost six games in a row and didn't score in any of them. In the end Frank Taylor got desperate and started dropping all the forwards. First Frank Bowyer and then myself and George Kelly! He tried just about every teenager we had at the club to see if they could provide a spark but nothing happened.

In the end we picked up five points in the last five games, but still ended up six points off a promotion place. Nottingham Forest went up that year and they won the FA Cup two years later, so it just shows what can happen if it all works out for you. I don't think we really recovered from that disappointment until Tony Waddington came along and began to change things around.

THERE AREN'T MANY people who have scored over 100 goals for Stoke. I understand there's only nine, and I'm honoured to be fifth on the list behind John Ritchie, Frank Bowyer, Freddie Steele and an old-timer called Charlie Wilson.

I was honoured to be selected to play for England on a tour of Africa in the summer of 1956. It was officially an FA squad because the South African authorities had recently instituted Apartheid, so we weren't called England and it meant I didn't win a full cap. We spent 10 weeks out there in South Africa and Rhodesia (now Zimbabwe). We had a great squad including the likes of a very young Bobby Charlton, Bobby Robson, Bedford Jezzard of Fulham, Gerry Hitchens from Aston Villa, Bill Perry, who'd scored the winning goal in the 1953 FA Cup final for Blackpool and West Ham's centre-half John Bond, who went on to become well known as a manager of Norwich and Manchester City. I was delighted to be included and am proud to have repsented my country at that level.

The game has changed so much these days. We were local boys, we felt so much closer to the club and to the supporters. Even though I lived at Crewe and was considered the outsider of the bunch, I was part of the area.

Things were very different in our day. I don't believe in all this warming up at two o'clock for a three o'clock kick off. No, no, no. It's a load of bloody rubbish. We just had a few stretches in the dressing room beforehand to loosen off, but you can't warm up an hour before a game, you tighten up again.

It's drummed into the players today that they have to be professional, but we had real characters in our day, like Ken Thomson and Bill Asprey, who really fancied himself as a ladies' man. The modern game doesn't have characters like that. A lot of today's game is slow motion. They pass it across all the time, in front of the defence. It's all slow stuff. It was that Ray Wilkins who started that. Ball retention? Very average if you ask me. It's so slow, across the midfield, then out to the wing. Nothing happening? Then back across the midfield and out to the other wing. It's all about not making mistakes. In our day it was about testing the other side, not waiting for them to drop a bollock!

The other thing that was special about that season was that it was groundsman Harry Lofill's 40th with the club. To think, he had first stuck his fork into the Victoria Ground turf in 1914, just before the First World War broke out! He used to tell us how he had put the drainage system under the Vic's turf in himself just after the first war and it was common even in my day for braziers to be used to thaw out the pitch after snowfall or a heavy frost.

He told us this story, I'll never know if it was true, but there was this one time when Stoke were playing West Brom at home. It was just after Harry had joined the club, so during the First World War, and they had these old wooden goalposts that hadn't been replaced for some time because of the war effort. They weren't very good and in fact the crossbar was joined in the middle, rather than being one long piece of wood. Anyway, during this game the West Brom keeper tipped a shot over the bar and then hung on to it, swinging on it for a few seconds. But because it was joined in the middle, the thing collapsed on him. Harry raced over to fix the goalposts and grabbed the nearest piece of wood he could find, strapping it on like a splint to bind the two pieces of bar together so the goal stood up and the game could continue. He stood admiring his handiwork, thinking what a good job he'd done and then realised that someone was tugging at his coat. He turned round to see this crippled youth, who could now not stand up because Harry had taken his crutch, which he'd put at the front of the terrace while he leant on the crush barrier! The poor bloke had to wait until the game was over to get his crutch back!

I'M STILL VERY fit and full of energy. In fact these days I often go up and watch local league football every other Saturday when Crewe aren't at home and every Sunday and act as ball boy as they don't have any of their own! I may be 74, but I can chase after a ball alright. Don Ratcliffe says that I run more now than when I used to play! But I was all about scoring goals. Goals meant everything to me during my career. It seems such a long time ago now.

DON RATCLIFFE: BORN 13 NOV 1934, NEWCASTLE-UNDER-LYME; 264 GAMES, 19 GOALS

Don Ratcliffe

Stoke City 2 Real Madrid 2
Centenary celebration match
Wednesday 24 April 1963

I SHOULD HAVE done National Service. I'd been in the first team since the age of 17 or 18 and when I got to 21 there was no avoiding it any more. After all, it was obligatory for all young men back in the 1950s and early '60s, but I got out of it. Unfit for duty. It was hilarious really because I was the fittest player at Stoke City in those days.

To give you an idea of how fit I was, when we were defending a corner I used to drop back on the left wing just outside our penalty area and our goalkeeper Jimmy O'Neill used to throw out the ball to me knowing I'd set off racing towards the corner flag to get a cross in as we counter-attacked. In those days I'd be running along the front of the Butler Street paddock and there were some gates at the end of the stand where it joined the Boothen End, past the corner flag and, as I raced up over the halfway line haring for the flagstick, the crowd all used to get up and shout, "Open the gates!" Time after time, they shouted it. They knew I would just keep running and running until the referee blew the whistle to end the game. That was me. Fit as hell.

The invalids and disabled people used to be positioned at the front of that stand and this one day there was a lad there who was very, very knock-kneed. I was having a bad game, but I forced a corner, and the ball ran off towards those gates. This young lad ran after the ball to get it. Knees everywhere. And he picked it up, but instead of giving it to me he put it straight on the corner flag and as he did the crowd shouted, "Let him take it!" Anyway I took it and I went and put it straight out! And the crowd all screamed, "Told you so!"

When it came to my medical to go into the Forces, I turned up to be assessed and it was Doc Crowe who was doing my medical. As it happened, he was the Stoke club doctor and a director at the time to boot. He took one look at me and said, "You'll go in the army, son, when they need 'em, not feed 'em. Grade Four. Sinusitis." And he signed me off as unfit!

I even played in the first team on the following Saturday!

I could run and run and run when I was a player. What annoys me is that people bang on about how fit they are today and how fast they are. Well I would like to see any of them that could live with me. I could go all day, and I was quick. I remember once against Barnsley, our forward George Kelly, Johnny King's striker partner, called for the ball. I sent a pass up the wing, the 'channel' they would call it today, expecting him to chase after it. But he had stopped, expecting the ball to feet. He moaned at me as the ball made its way towards the goal line and I thought, "Sod this" and legged it after it.

All the Barnsley defenders had stopped too as they had seen that no one was chasing the ball down. The keeper had given it up as a lost cause too thinking it was going out for a goal kick, but I knew that I hadn't hit it hard enough to go out. So I ran as hard as I could and caught the ball up – a 60 yard pass to myself! By this time the defenders had woken up to what was going on, but I'd got a start on them and brought the ball in from the wing, took on the goalkeeper and slipped it past him to score.

The crowd took to me and they used to gee me up by shouting, "Rat-A-Tat-Tat" really loud. I knew that they were encouraging me to get going, get stuck in and get past the full-back and it did wonders for me.

I WAS A scallywag really as a kid. I came from a fairly deprived background as a miner's son and I was always up to something when I was younger. There was this local grocer's that I used to pop over the back wall, grab as many empty bottles as I could and then go in through the front door and take them back and claim the money on them. It used to be threepence a bottle.

I was a swimmer and a gymnast at school. I was good and I won lots of awards as a kid and it stood me in good stead for my football career, because I had stamina from swimming and flexibility and muscle power from the gymnastics.

When I got to Stoke we used to play all sorts of tricks on each other. Jimmy O'Neill was a scamp. He once went round all the butchers in Newcastle at Christmas and ordered 27 turkeys in my name and bloody sold them on. And I was going in these various butchers and they were saying, "When are you settling your bill then?" I had to tell Waddo in the end and Stoke paid the bill, and stopped it out of his wages!

We'd also see him thumbing a lift on his day off. If we weren't playing on a Tuesday we'd have the day off and there would be Jimmy thumbing a lift to a racecourse – Stoke City's goalkeeper thumbing a lift! We were then on around £25 a week, just after the lifting of the maximum wage, and he would think nothing of gambling a week's wages or more. He was a mad gambler on the horses. You know what the Irish are like!

I was always getting myself into scrapes. I lived about two miles from the ground and travelled in on the bus every day, but on a matchday of course, it would be full of supporters. This one day I waited for the bus, but it was late and then when it came it was packed. Absolutely jam packed. And I couldn't get on it. So I ran all the way to the ground. I didn't get there until twenty to three and Frank Taylor, the manager, wanted to know where I'd been! I daren't tell him I'd run two miles from home to the ground!

WE USED TO have some great fun – and out on the pitch during the game too, mind. I got fetched down in this game and I was lying on the floor with my boot off after the foul and I'd hurt myself, so I didn't get up straight away, and Ken Thomson, who was our centre-half, skipper and all round top man, jogged over, picked up my boot and threw it into the crowd! And we only had two pairs of boots in those days, one with studs and one mouldeds. So there was me shouting at the paddock crowd asking them to throw me the boot back! It took bloody ages! "Give me my boot back!" It was a while, but it did eventually come back.

He also developed an interesting way of forcing you to get up quickly when you were injured. If you went down, he'd come over and help you up, except as he did so he'd stick his middle finger up your bum! I remember the first time he goosed me even now. After that every time I went down, he'd come over and the crowd thought he was helping me and giving me some sympathy, but he wasn't. I made sure I got up sharpish!

The game was packed full of characters like that – and entertaining footballers. I always remember playing against Len Shackleton – he was known as The Clown Prince of Soccer - in my first season. I was playing wing-half to mark him out of the game as I was considered the one who could chase him down. But I couldn't get near him. He stood on top of the ball enticing me in. Cheeky beggar. Of course I lunged in and he played a one-two off the corner flag to try and beat me! He nearly got there as well, but the ball just went out.

When Tony Waddington became manager he used to love to have some great players in his team, mixed in with all of us kids and hard workers. He brought in Dennis Viollet, Jackie Mudie, and Jimmy McIlroy, who were all fantastic.

Dennis Viollet was one hell of a player. He's still the record goalscorer in one season at Manchester United, and Waddo did fantastic to get him to come to Stoke. He could do anything with a ball. I remember this one game I passed him this ball in the box. He was in a tight spot with a defender at his back and the keeper coming out to meet him. He turned on a sixpence. He'd got a tiny bit of space now, but he couldn't see any way past the goalkeeper, so as he rushed out at Dennis's feet, Dennis put his foot under the ball and lifted it over the keeper, and tried to hurdle him! The goalkeeper took his back leg, so technically it was a penalty, but the ref didn't give it. Eddie Stuart comes charging over and picks Dennis up from the mud and says, "You chicken", because he thought Dennis had bottled out of going in hard on the keeper to force the ball home. Eddie then threw Dennis back down into the mud and as he scraped himself up again he looked at me and said, "If you can't hear the music, you can't play the drums." He was on about Eddie Stuart being stupid and not realising what had gone on! What a player!

Then there was Eddie Clamp. Talk about a character. Clampy was probably the hardest man I knew. At corners I used to put the ball down to take them and look up to see what he was up to, because I knew that he would be on the lookout for whoever had annoyed him that game. If he found him, he'd wait to see when the ref was looking over at me and the ball and then headbutt the player. Well, I knew what he was going to do, so when I saw him going near a player I'd quickly take the corner, so the referee was definitely looking my way and wouldn't see what Eddie was up to!

I remember this one time we went down to Cardiff, and they had this little wing-half called Colin Webster, who used to play for Manchester United and was one of the original Busby Babes. He had broken our full-back George Bourne's leg while playing for United's reserves. It was an injury which finished George and Eddie had heard about this and decided that retribution was in order. Bear in mind that this incident had happened about seven years earlier, well before Eddie was at the club.

Anyway, at half-time we were walking down the tunnel at Swansea's old ground, the Vetch Field. In the tunnel there was this girder at head height, I'd say at about 6ft 2in. It was obvious as they'd put a sign on it saying 'Please mind your head'. As we came off the pitch, I was walking behind Webster, with Eddie behind me. Next minute, Clampy grabbed me by the back of the neck, picked me up and put me behind him so he could be next to Webster. He taps Webster on the back and as he turns round Eddie's smacked him with his head. His nose was spread all over his face.

We went into the dressing rooms and the referee comes in and says, "Mr Clamp. I've heard that you have head-butted Webster."

"No, sir. He banged his head on that girder."

Well, Webster was only about 5ft 6in!

The referee went out and Waddo's sitting there, head in hands, saying, "Eddie what are you on about, he's banged his head on the girder? What did he do jump up and head it?!"

We used to train up and down Trentham Hills. Running up and down as hard as we could to build up stamina and fitness. At the end of a run, Waddo would keep me at the bottom of the hill and start the rest of them about halfway up and he'd shout up to them, "Every one he passes is back this afternoon!" And I used to go past each and every one of them! They used to try to kick shit out of me as I hared past them!

We used to have some fun training. I remember I was practising free kicks once and hit this one from outside the area incredibly hard. It hit the bar in front of the big old Town End terrace and came down so hard that it buried itself in the mud. It was that muddy at the Vic that the ball actually disappeared!

There was another occasion when I had a bit of a fracas with Bill Asprey. He was quite conceited, loved himself really, and that annoyed me. But we grew up at Stoke together as we were the same age. One day he kicked me in training and I put him out of the game for three weeks by kicking him back. We were playing five-a-side and he took this great kick at me in proper boots, not trainers. So I retaliated. Then trainer Len Graham comes over after we'd finished training and says, "The boss wants to see you." So I went to Waddo and he said, "You know Bill Asprey's going to be out for three weeks?"

"Yes," I said

"Well, you're fined £5."

I was only on about £12 per week. So I'd barely got anything left!

I LOVED TONY Waddington. He was really good for me as we started at the club on the same night and as he got on, I got on. We progressed together through part-timers, A team and reserves and I'm sure he told Frank Taylor to take a chance on me in the first team. When Waddo became manager, he would always make sure you were alright in your home life and he'd got pretty much every aspect of things covered. I remember this one day, I was sitting in the dressing room and I needed a few tickets. We used to get two or three as of right anyway, but on this occasion I was feeling pretty down because loads of people had asked me to get tickets for the Real Madrid game and they were like gold dust. So in comes Waddo and he sees I've got a long face and he says, "What's up, Don?"

"I need some tickets, Boss. I'm a local lad and this is a big, big game."

"How many?"

"35!"

He just laughed and then said, "Come into my office."

He got out some tickets and counted out 35 of them and handed them over to me, saying, "Now then, you'd better perform."

I said, "I'll kill for you tonight, Boss."

What a feller!

There was another occasion when Waddo got me into trouble, though. It was the opening day of the 1963/64 season after we got promoted and we had Spurs at home. Waddo played me at wing-half against a certain Dave Mackay and told me to, "Tip him up." Now when Waddo said that, what he meant was, "kick hell out of him". Mackay was a hard man and I kicked shit out of him. But he didn't respond. I remember he played a one-two and as he went for the return pass I just kicked him. And he barely broke stride. Then, about two minutes later, bloody hell he nearly cut me in half! He really, really did me. So I'm on the floor and I'm moaning to the referee, because I wasn't quite as hard as he was, and he came over to me and pulled out this white handkerchief. I don't know where he got it from, but he handed me this handkerchief and he said, "Now then, you didnae like that, did ye?"

Talking of hard men, I remember the first time I played against Liverpool's Tommy Smith. We were lining up before kick-off and I was playing right-wing against him at left-back. As we were getting ready, Smith shouted to me, "I hear you're fast."

"Yes, that's right."

"Not without one leg you're not"!

Leeds had a hard team in those days. Don Revie demanded it of them. I remember giving this full-back a tremendous chasing. I can't remember his name now, but it was at the Vic and I kept beating him and Revie was getting very worked up about it on the sidelines. This full-back got the ball and set off up the wing to attack and I chased him down and slid across the usual Victoria Ground mud to put him and the ball out of play. Revie came charging out of his box, with his neck muscles all bulging and the veins on his head all standing out, to scream at the player, "I told you to give him a good kicking." He was pointing at me, of course. And the guy replied, "I'm trying, but I can't catch him"! I was pleased with that as they'd obviously picked me out as a player to try to deal with.

OF COURSE EVERYTHING changed at Stoke the day Stan Matthews came back to the club. The story goes that a player called Dennis Wilshaw, who had played for Wolves and won several England caps including scoring four goals at Wembley against Scotland in 195??, broke his leg really badly at Newcastle. I remember that well; this centre-half did him, came over the ball and shattered the bone in his calf because Dennis was a serious goal threat, even though he was coming to the end of his career. We called him 'Mr Nearly' at Stoke because, despite the fact he'd been a top player, his first touch wasn't that great.

On this occasion I had passed the ball to him and he didn't control it first time, giving the centre-half, Billy Thompson his name was, a chance to put a hard tackle in. So I was very close by and I can remember the bone sticking out of the back of his leg. It was bent in the shape of a U. It was the worst thing I ever saw on a football pitch. I actually felt sick.

Anyway, Dennis was finished, but he kept coming down to the club for treatment to get him at least to walk properly again, although his leg ended up about half an inch shorter. After his rehab work he'd come up to the training ground and see how we were all getting on. This one day he was chatting with Waddo and, having been older himself when he came to the club, mentioned that he thought it would be a good idea to bring Stanley Matthews back to Stoke. Waddo obviously agreed because that's exactly what he did.

Stan had been languishing in Blackpool's reserves after a pay dispute. He was already 46, so way past the age that any other player would have retired at, and yet here he was still in demand and still able to pull in the crowds. It worked perfectly for Stoke. The crowds packed into the Victoria Ground to see his debut against Huddersfield in October 1961 and the magic seemed to return.

Stan's signing did wonders for me. I was captain of the club at the time and during the close season I'd re-negotiated my contract, so that it included a bonus for the entire squad if aggregate attendances topped 250,000, which for 21 home games meant an average of 11,900. For every 1,000 over that figure £10 would be pooled and we'd all have our share based on the number of first team appearances we made.

Well, the minute Stan came back the place took off. For his first game we had over 35,000 there and the aggregate attendances topped 300,000. It was the best average gate for donkey's years. We cleaned up!

His return helped raise the profile of the club again and Waddo was able to bring in the likes of Viollet and McIlroy for the 1962/63 season. He'd already brought in other players such as goalkeeper Jimmy O'Neill and Blackpool forward Jackie Mudie and we got the nickname of 'The Old Crocks' - even though players like myself, Tony Allen, Bill Asprey and Eric Skeels were under 25! The thing was the players that came in were big names, high-profile, so the name stuck.

Skeelsy, of course, has made the most appearances of anyone in a Stoke shirt. But I always tease him that he never wanted the ball. If I had it in a tight spot I'd be looking to get rid of it and he'd be inside me saying, "Not me, not me!" But his game wasn't to pass the ball. He was a tackler, a worker. He was a good player, but he was solid and you need players like that in a team. You could understand why Waddo kept him in the team for so long.

I HAVE CHOSEN the Real Madrid game as my special game – there was no doubt in my mind. The thing I remember the most was playing with Di Stefano, Puskas and Gento because they were gods. They'd won the European Cup five times in a row.

I remember the kick-off clear as day. Di Stefano just tapped it to Puskas and he flipped it up with his right foot and then hit it on the volley with his left foot – he had the most unbelievable left foot. The ball flew the length of the field and landed on top of the crossbar. Jimmy O'Neill would never have got it. Straight from the kick-off!

I thought, "Bloody Hell!"

And Dennis Viollet ran over and said to me, "We're in fucking trouble here!"

Dennis also said that to me on one other occasion. It was first time we played Leeds after they got relegated in 1960 and John Charles had just returned to the club from his time in Italy ??. He had oiled himself up, had his shorts rolled up high, as he did, and he was massive. He looked like a great, big, black bouncer on a club door. He looked tremendous. Quite frightening. And as we kicked off, Dennis came over to me again and said, "We're in trouble here!"

And do you know we played that day and Charles scored two in the first half and then went and played centre-half and we lost 3-1.

Anyway, the Real Madrid game was a huge game for the club to celebrate its centenary. It was big news in the country at the time as we had Real Madrid over here and the last game they'd played in Britain had been the incredible 7-3 victory over Eintracht Frankfurt in the 1960 European Cup final at Hampden Park. Having all these big name players over meant that the eyes of the nation were on Stoke. I remember the build-up in the media was all about these great players that would entertain everyone with wonderful football – and I thought, hang on a minute, I can play too you know. Di Stefano was 37 by the way, so he was no spring chicken, although admittedly Stan beat him hands down in those stakes, being 48 and just about to win his second Footballer of the Year award, 15 years after winning the inaugural one!

Memories still lingered of the time Madrid had played a similar friendly at Wolves in 195?? and lost 3-2 at Molineux, and they had after all lost the previous season's European Cup final 5-3 to Benfica – so perhaps they were an ailing team! They certainly didn't lack stars. Ruiz, Di Stefano, Gento, Puskas and Santamaria were all among the world's best.

They had been on a tour of European opposition such as Bordeaux and Hamburg in the preceding weeks, after turning down all offers of overseas friendlies until they had clinched their third successive Spanish League title – a feat never before achieved. So this was a special side. They'd beaten all their previous opponents without conceding a goal!

I remember before the game the famous president Don Santiago Bernabau, who created the Real Madrid we all know, and built their stadium which is named after him, said, during the reception the night before the game at the North Stafford Hotel where they were staying, "This visit to Stoke is the one of the highlights of my life"! He obviously hadn't called in at Chell Heath or Fegg Hayes on his way into the city!! He meant the club that had discovered Stan Matthews, of course, and it was incredible how Stan's name was known around the world. His arrival really did change the club beyond all recognition.

The timing of the game was good as we were top of the league having gone on a great run since the long break, which an incredibly hard winter hard forced us to take. We hadn't played from the end of December to the start of March, but we'd done really well since the thaw and were confident of going up.

62,000 had seen us at fellow promotion challengers Sunderland on Good Friday, while 42,00 had turned up for the return on Easter Monday at the Vic. We'd won that match 2-1 thanks to two Dennis Viollet goals and we were now looking nailed on for promotion. We could relax and take the Madrid game as a proper celebration match.

As it was Gento was injured and didn't play, but aside from that Madrid played their full team. After that frightening opening to the match, Madrid controlled things really and it was up to us to get amongst them. That was my job and I relished it along with Eddie Clamp. I got well and truly stuck in. I read the match report from the following day's *Sentinel* recently and it describes me as "getting stuck in in his own inimitable style"!

Madrid were class, though, and kept control for much of the first half, but they only scored once. Di Stefano put a header wide from a few yards out, but then the?? broke free and raced clear to hammer home past Jimmy O'Neill. I think we did well to restrict them to one goal in the first half and after we regrouped a bit at half-time, and they made some changes to their team, we came right back into it.

Straight after the restart, Dennis Viollet picked up the ball on the edge of the area from a Jimmy McIlroy pass, beat one player and hit a shot which took a bit of a deflection which helped it into the far corner of the net. Then came my crowning moment. The full-back I was up against, ??, really wasn't very good. Maybe he was just having an off night, but I was skinning him for fun. Time after time. I beat him again a few minutes after our first goal and crossed for Jimmy McIlroy to score. Now we were suddenly 2-1 up against the great Real Madrid. Fantastic!

Ron Andrew had come on as centre-half in the first half because of an injury to Eddie Stuart. Ron was still a bit green and he got well and truly done by Puskas, who produced a lovely piece of skill in the area and had Ron flying in to tackle a ball that wasn't there any more. So they got a penalty. Jimmy O'Neill tells this great story about that spot-kick. On the afternoon before the match we'd all popped down to watch Madrid training and Puskas was there practising penalties. He cracked every single shot low and hard into the left hand corner of the goal. Six spot-kicks. When it came to the penalty in the match, Jimmy thought he had it covered. He knew exactly where it was going, so as Puskas hit the ball he flung himself to his right. But Puskas simply rolled the ball into the other corner, leaving Jimmy somewhat red-faced!

Stan had a wonderful game that night. He always raised himself for the big game and he played beautifully that night, causing the Spaniards all sorts of problems. He tired towards the end of games, though, as he was obviously getting on and Madrid missed a couple of chances to win the match when Amancia went clean through. The first time he shot just wide and the second time Jimmy O'Neill saved at his feet. Bueno then hit the post, just as Puskas had earlier. But we survived and I think in the last ten minutes both sides settled for the draw. It was a cracking match and a great result.

THE HIGH PROFILE of the fixture meant that England coach Walter Winterbottom came to see the game – among over 300 invited guests. And fortunately for me, great team that Madrid were, they had that poor full-back, or at least I'd beat him for fun all game, anyway. I'd played really well and had lots of good write-ups in the press afterwards, so I was pleased, but then Waddo called me into his office the day after the game and said that Walter had been impressed with me. Apparently Winterbottom had been asking where I'd been all this time, as he'd been looking for a player like me to play for England!

Shortly afterwards the English League were due to play the Scottish League at Highbury in one of the inter-league matches they used to have, and Bobby Charlton of Manchester United was due to play outside-left (Charlton began his career at Old Trafford as a left winger and didn't move inside until the arrival of George Best), but he got injured the weekend before and so I was put on standby. Waddo phoned me and said, "Winterbottom wants you to go down to Arsenal tomorrow and take your boots." I just started to get excited when he phoned back a couple of hours later to say that Charlton was OK and would be playing, so not to bother going.

Anyway, the next day Charlton broke down and failed his fitness test before the game. But I wasn't there, I was still in Stoke, so the Arsenal outside-right, his name was Wright, got a game instead, because he was Johnny on the spot. It should have been me. And I never got a chance to play again. How unlucky can you get!

I'm not saying I would have gone on to win a cap, but it would have been nice to play!

I PLAYED IN nine positions in my Stoke career. I didn't play at centre-half or in goal, and Waddo said he could have sold me in every one. In fact at the time of all those older players being in the team, I was actually more or less the only one he could sell, apart from perhaps Tony Allen. Waddo called me into his room and asked me to see the Middlesbrough manager Raich Carter, who was a very, very famous player. I did so and had a good chat and everything, but when I got back I saw Waddo and said, "I'm not going." He told me that he needed me to go as he needed the cash for two or three new players and that he'd agreed a fee of £27,500 with Middlesbrough, whereas in actual fact I was only worth £10,000!

Then Waddo said that if I went he'd give me £1,000. Now a new car then was only around £600, so I bit the bullet and agreed to go. Looking back I wish I hadn't as I never really wanted to leave Stoke, but it all seemed to make sense at the time.

He used the money to bring in right-half Calvin Palmer, goalkeeper Lawrie Leslie from West Ham and George Kinnell from Aberdeen. He also signed a young centre-forward called John Ritchie from non-league Kettering Town for a snip at £2,500. So I suppose from his point of view he got a great deal out of me. Perhaps I should claim the credit!

I suppose I was lucky in a sense because I had two benefits at Stoke. I didn't even have to ask for them, unlike most players who had to pester the management to get theirs. I got £750 after five years' service and then after ten years' service I got another £1,000. It was a funny system as you didn't get that money as of right, just if the club wanted to give it to you.

So I went to Middlesbrough and then on to Darlington and Crewe. I won promotion with both of the last to clubs, but nothing was as special as playing for my hometown team and that magical night against Madrid was a very special occasion indeed.

TONY ALLEN: BORN 27 NOVEMBER 1939, STOKE-ON-TRENT; 483 GAMES, 4 GOALS

Tony Allen

Chelsea 0 Stoke City 1

League Division Two

Saturday 11 May 1963

MY DREAM WAS playing football. I was useless at school. Honestly. I hadn't got a bloody clue. So my time at Stoke was the best 15 years I ever spent. To win promotion and then get capped for England was incredible. I thought I was dreaming.

I suppose my greatest game should have been my first international cap, but I'm going for the game that effectively won us promotion and the Second Division title in 1963, when we won 1-0 at Chelsea. The atmosphere that day, I've never seen anything like it. Not for league matches. There was 66,000 packed into Stamford Bridge. It was electrifying. And we played fantastic. I think it's the best performance I've ever seen a Stoke City side play. And nobody more than Stanley Matthews – at the age of 48 – because he was up against Eddie McCreadie at left-back and Ron Harris at left-half and for the first ten minutes they kicked him. They just kicked and kicked at him. Black and blue. And he just got up – a bloke of nearly 50 – he got up off the floor and took them to the bloody cleaners! He really did. Honestly. He was magnificent.

WHEN I WAS young, I used to play for Stoke-on-Trent schoolboys, playing in the English schools trophy and we'd done very well. I don't know what's happening in terms of bringing on the youths these days, either in the city or at the club. There doesn't seem to be any youth development, they certainly don't seem to be getting into the first team. It did wonders for me, though, got me noticed. We had a good side. One or two of the players from my era signed for the Vale, people like Colin Bates. It developed us as players, playing against the best teams from around the country at the age of 13, 14 and 15.

I was lucky to tell you the truth. In school holiday time we went training twice a week and there was a little fellow there, a teacher, named Bill Organ. He was only about 5ft nothing. He was a sports teacher at one of the Longton schools and could he shout?! Blimey – you wouldn't argue with him. Well, this one day, for some reason, I didn't go down training. I don't know why I didn't go, but I didn't turn up. Anyway, Bill found me playing with my mates in their back yard, two or three doors down the road from my house. And he grabbed me and yanked me out of the yard and said, "Get your boots. We're off." He could have washed his hands of me, but he didn't, and I never missed another training session. Then we played Mid-Cheshire and there were scouts from several league clubs there watching, West Brom were one, but Stoke and Vale came in for me.

I was a Vale man actually. From where I lived in Northwood, I used to walk through Hanley Deep Pit to go watch them play as a kid; every home match, never missed one. And I should have signed for the Vale. I met Freddie Steele, a former Stoke legend, but then the Vale manager, with my Dad. And the forms were on the desk ready for me to sign. Remember they were my team, and they were offering me terms. But for some reason, and again I don't know why, don't ask me because I really don't know, I turned to my Dad and said, "I'm going to sign for Stoke." So I did.

I think it was the best thing to do, and I don't mean that to do Vale down, but I never looked back really. I got into the first team at 18 when John McCue retired. Frank Taylor gave me the chance, although I think it was on Tony Waddington's recommendation because he was the reserve team coach. I'd been playing in the Birmingham League against the likes of Villa and West Brom and Birmingham since the age of 16, once I'd signed for Stoke. It was great experience.

Frank had got frustrated with how the team had begun the 1957/58 season and he had two experienced, but ageing full-backs in John McCue and Frank Mountford, who were both in their late 30s. The team didn't start the season particularly well and got hammered 5-3 at Bristol Rovers and he decided to change things and I got a chance. I travelled to Doncaster with the first team and they didn't tell me that I was going to play. I didn't find out until just before the kick-off that I was playing – just as well really as I didn't have time to get nervous. We won 1-0 and I didn't look back from there.

The older players did a lot to help me. Frank Mountford taught me a lot about full-back play, more than John McCue, because John was a part-timer. I also had a lot of help from Frank Bowyer and Ken Thomson, the captain. Before that first game Frank Taylor told me, "When you get the ball, hit it up the line for Johnny King." Well, we went on the pitch and just before kick-off Frank Bowyer came over and said, "When you get the ball, I'll be ten yards inside you. Give it me and you'll be alright." So I did, and Frank used to get the ball and turn and hit these long passes to bring the wingers into play. He made my debut easy.

Ken Thomson was a great stopper, probably the best centre-half I played with. Not may got past him. He was the captain as well and dominated the centre of the pitch. He made life easy for me and I just fitted in well to the team.

I was always sick before I played. In the dressing room I was sick and then my nerves would calm down. Throughout my career that's how it went. As a full-back I was near the crowd all the time, and you could hear everything, and if you did anything wrong - crikey! Some of the older players, that had been there quite a while, they used to give them some stick. I think being a young local lad, they took to me, so I was spared early on in my career.

WE USED TO go for a pre-match meal at the North Staffs hotel by the station and walk down to the ground. And this one day we were walking along and Stan was in front of me and he was walking strangely. He was dragging his heels and I thought, "He's walking funny." Anyway when we got into the dressing room, I saw him sit down and take his shoes off and then I saw that he'd got lead in the heels. He'd put lead in there to weigh him down, so when he took it out he felt he was running on air. Incredible he was. You wouldn't believe what it did to us and the crowd when his name was on the teamsheet. It's amazing what just a name did. It intimidated opponents. I remember that first game against Huddersfield. Ray Wilson, who of course won the World Cup with England in 1966, couldn't go near him because he said he knew he'd be lynched if he did!

I remember Stan training. There used to be a low white wall all the way around the Vic and Stan would chalk a cross on the wall and practise hitting the ball against it. Every time he'd hit it eight times out of ten at least. He was so accurate in his passing and crossing. A perfectionist.

Of course as a dribbler, no one could touch him. He used to have snakehips. He used to shimmy at people as he went towards them, he had quick feet and then he would explode over the first three yards and go past the player. Then they couldn't catch him over the next 20. He used to slow everything down and then go. Quick as a flash. It was like drawing the defender into a mousetrap and then bang – he'd be off. They couldn't get near him.

Of course as a left-back I often faced Stan in training and I upset him once to tell you the truth. We were playing first team defence against first team attack with the reserves filling in the gaps and it was a foot deep in sludge on the practice pitch over the back of the Vic. Stan went past me and I slide-tackled him into the sludge. He didn't like it, but I didn't like him taking the piss out of me, because he would take the piss if he could. He loved humiliating full-backs and a lot of his game was based on mentally destroying his opponent. Anyway, I slid in and took the ball and Stan off the pitch and into this deep mud. And he got up slowly and gave me this look. Withering isn't the word. And he just got up and walked off. Walked off the pitch and into the dressing rooms. He really wasn't happy. And I thought, "I've gone for a burton here"! He never mentioned it after that and it took him a fortnight to speak to me! But I wasn't having him going past me.

We had some characters in our team, Eddie Stuart and Eddie Clamp for example. I wasn't hard at all, despite that tackle on Matthews, but those two were properly hard. Don Ratcliffe was special. He was mad, mind. I remember the bath in the old stand at the Vic. It was about 15ft long and three feet deep and we'd soak in it after the games, but Ratter would do stupid things in it. I remember we'd egg him on to stand on the window sill, just above the rim of the bath and somersault into it. Remember it wasn't that deep and it was bloody hard if you hit your head – but he'd do it. He'd been a gymnast as a kid, so he could manage it without hitting the side of this head on the bath. He was proper crackers with some of the things he did!

I WASN'T A goalscorer. I only scored four. I waited four years to score my first goal and then two came along at once; one against Leeds and one against Leicester. We were 1-0 down against Leeds and I picked a ball up inside our half and went forward and nobody came towards me, so I carried on. I got inside the penalty box, and I played a one-two with Jackie Mudie to get past Jackie Charlton and he put me in to shoot past Tommy Younger. I did it again five minutes later. I went for a one-two and Charlton came with me expecting the same move, and Mudie instead turned on the ball and scored the winner.

But my first goal was against actually against Leicester and I scored past Gordon Banks in the FA Cup. We won 5-2 and Stan scored that night. When Gordon came to Stoke, Stan used to always tease him about having a 47-year-old scoring past him!

Then I waited another six years before I got two more goals; one against Watford in the cup and one against Southampton in the league. Actually I think I scored more own goals in my career! But then that's an occupational hazard for a defender.

I played 126 games on the trot early in my career until I got injured, so I must have been doing something right. That doesn't happen these days, unless you're Frank Lampard of course! I never really used to get injured. I certainly never pulled a muscle. My only major injury was having my cartilage out, which kept me out for six weeks. I don't understand how they get all these injuries these days. They have strained calves and groin muscles – we never used to have those.

People called the way I played stylish, I wasn't particularly quick, but I could read the play and anticipate where the ball was going, so

I could intercept. That got me noticed, I think. I would mark behind people and as the ball was played up to the forward, I would nip round them and take it off them. I used to think a yard ahead of the others. I wasn't a hard tackler like McCue or Pejic. I had two good feet and could pass the ball well.

I got called up for one England youth match against Romania at Tottenham and I didn't do bad, I'm not saying I was brilliant, but I did quite well. I never thought anything more than to keep playing football for Stoke City – that was my No. 1 project. I never heard any more from England for the rest of the season, but then the under-23s came in and asked me to play and that was with big name players. I played at Sheffield Wednesday against Czechoslovakia and I then played eight straight matches and I improved with every match.

We went on a pre-season tour to Italy and Germany and we beat the Italians 3-0 in Turin, which was a fantastic result. That was the first time I was frightened of playing football. In the first five minutes I tackled their winger and fouled him. Well, the whistles and jeers I got – unbelievable. But we played really well that day and won easily and the fans turned on their team at the end of the game and whistled, jeered and threw their seats at them. It was incredible. They don't like losing!

After the match we were in the shower and John Charles, who was at Juventus at the time, came in the dressing room. He was enormous, the size of his shoulders! He said, "Tremendous performance, well done." And he stayed for half an hour and encouraged us.

Even though we'd been a while before we left the ground, as we left on the coach the Italian fans were trying to tip it over! They'd waited for us and they really weren't happy about losing!

But then we moved on to Germany, to Bochum, and we drew 2-2. I must have had a good game then because the following day I was in the papers and they'd all given me nine out of ten. It was great. But if you can't play with great players like Jimmy Armfield at right-back, Bobby Charlton and Trevor Smith at centre-half then you shouldn't be there. It was easy. Tremendous players they were.

I played for the Football League four times as well and then, out of the blue, I got a call-up. I found out about it in a strange way. This lad called Tony Knapp came over to me after an under-23 game against Hungary at Everton when we won 2-0, and he said, "You're going to be playing for the full team next game." And I said, "Who are you kidding?" But I was selected. I couldn't believe it. I was happy doing what I was doing, but I got picked and I was chuffed to death. I had that many letters wishing me well. It was fantastic – and my dad was more proud than me.

My debut was against Wales. We drew 1-1 and then beat Ireland and lost to Sweden 3-2. We had the likes of Ronnie Clayton and Bryan Douglas in that team, plus Ron Flowers, then Brian Clough and Jimmy Greaves up front. Not a bad side. It was a tremendous pleasure to play in that team.

APART FROM MY international debut there were two other matches which really stand out for me at Stoke. The first was when we beat reigning FA Cup holders Aston Villa in the third round the following season. We drew twice with them and then beat them in a second replay at Wolverhampton. I remember that game. It had snowed and the Molineux pitch was incredibly icy. The trainers had knocked nails into the studs in our boots because it was that icy. We were slipping and sliding around the pitch after a few minutes because the nails got rammed up into the boots! It's amazing they got away with that because you'd think it would cut someone in half! But you could do that kind of thing in those days. It was criminal really because if you caught someone on the shin you'd rip them to pieces. You didn't have to wear shin pads in those days remember. Anyway, over 37,000 saw us defeat the Villa 2-0, with Tim Coleman and Bobby Cairns scoring the goals.

We went back to Wolverhampton for a second replay three years later, but that wasn't quite as auspicious. We'd drawn twice against Aldershot – two goalless draws, which was quite embarrassing. Thankfully we beat them 3-0 at Molineux.

The other match I remember well was when we beat Middlesbrough with Brian Clough 3-1 in the FA Cup. Cloughie was a great goalscorer, but he never did anything against Stoke.

I don't think he ever scored against us. He couldn't get past Ken Thomson. During that particular game Dennis Wilshaw had a great match. He scored a hat-trick and then got fed up with the amount of moaning that Clough was doing because his team were getting hammered and he was getting no change out of Thommo once again. Anyway Dennis was normally a really calm, professional sort of fellow, but this day Clough had annoyed him and he fouled him and then delayed Clough taking the free kick by walking off with the ball. Clough moaned to the ref and so Dennis threw the ball back to him, but to the side so that Clough had to walk across and then bend over to pick it up. Unbeknown to Cloughie, Dennis had followed the ball and as Clough picked it up, Dennis planted a big kick right up his backside, sending him flying!

The FA Cup was a great competition. We used to get great crowds and I loved to be able to take on the big boys and have a good cup run. It's not the same now with so much importance placed on the league..

We had a couple of embarrassments in the competition. I remember playing Walsall in 1966 and Bobby Irvine brought down Howard Reilly for a penalty. Then we attacked all game, but we couldn't score and they broke away and scored in the last minute and we lost 2-0 at home. They were in Division Three at the time and we were in Division One. I'd prefer to forget that one actually.

BUT IN THAT promotion season of 1962/63, our forward line was the oldest in the world, I think – there was Stan, then Dennis Viollet, Jimmy McIlroy, Jackie Mudie and the youngster, Don Ratcliffe. They must have had an average age of about 37!

Tony Waddington had brought in all these older, more experienced players and it really paid off. Earlier, he'd also brought in an inside-forward from Preston called Tommy Thompson, who'd played for England. He had this pair of football boots that looked like he had clogs on! Then there was winger Jimmy Adam from Aston Villa too. They arrived in 1961, after Waddo had tried some youngsters in his first season, such as Peter Bullock, who was the youngest player ever to play for Stoke, and Peter Ford. He also gave chances to people like Gerry Bridgwood, a winger, who didn't quite make it either, and Ron Andrew, a young centre-half, who played quite a few games, but was inexperienced. There were lots of others given a chance in a game or two as Tony scrabbled around for a team, but it wasn't until Jackie Mudie arrived just before deadline day in 1961, that things started to click. You gave Jackie a chance and he scored. Simple as that.

We didn't do very well at all with all those youngsters in the side that 1960/61 season, in fact we only stayed up by three points, but things gradually got better at the start of the new season. Tommy came in and scored a lot of goals (13 before Christmas). Two of those came on the day a certain Stan Matthews returned to Stoke to galvanise the club into action. We beat Huddersfield 3-0 that game and it seemed set in the stars that we would go on to do things.

We still hadn't got enough experience in the team in 1961/62 and we finished eighth in the Second Division, but Waddo used Stan's presence to bring in these fantastic players for the next season. In came Eddie Stuart and Eddie Clamp, who had both been integral to the Wolves team which had dominated English football in the late 1950s and won the FA Cup in 1960. That summer also saw Dennis Viollet arrive from Manchester United. He really made us play football. We passed the ball around and if we lost it we would get back and defend. Simple stuff, but we had enough good players to keep the ball, pass it around and score goals. Waddo just knew who to buy – look at Peter Dobing and George Eastham, who came after we'd won promotion. What a pair of players they were. Absolute class.

EVERYONE REMEMBERS THE winter of that 1962/63 season which kept the whole country snowbound for two months. It never thawed once in Stoke in that whole time. It was incredible. We had our games called off two or three days in advance because there was no chance of getting them on. It meant fixtures piled up and it could have jeopardised the bid for promotion, but we actually won seven out of eight games once we resumed playing.

We spent the whole time training while we couldn't play, but it was frustrating not being able to play games. We used to have snowball fights – it was always Ratter who started that, because he was crackers. Later on Maurice Setters and Taffy Vernon (Roy Vernon) came along and they were mad as well.

I used to room with Taffy and as you went to bed and turned the light out, all you used to see was the end of this cigarette glowing as he puffed on it. And then first thing in the morning you'd see it too; glowing reddy-orange above his covers. He smoked some cigarettes!

SO IN APRIL 1963 we were sitting pretty at the top of the Second Division with games in hand. Of course after the Real Madrid celebrations following the Centenary game, which went on long into the night, the only way was down, and we crashed to a surprise home defeat to Middlesbrough the following Saturday. Dennis Viollet had got injured against Madrid and we missed him badly. He actually missed the next three games and we lost the lot. We got stuffed 5-2 at Newcastle and then, embarrassingly lost 3-2 at home to Scunthorpe United would you believe. Hardly promotion form.

The Newcastle game was embarrassing too. We were 2-0 up after 18 minutes thanks to two goals by Jimmy McIlroy, who got on the end of some wonderful flowing moves. That should have seen us home and dry. But in four incredible minutes before half-time the game turned completely on its head. We conceded a penalty when Eddie Clamp brought down Hilley, and then a ridiculous equaliser. That goal was my fault. A long ball bounced between myself and Jimmy O'Neill and we clattered into each other in trying to clear it. I ended up heading it past Jimmy and towards the goal, leaving Alan Suddick to prod it over the line.

Suddick gave me a huge problem that night. I didn't get a chasing from many wingers, but he gave me one that night if I'm honest. There was a guy at Orient called Phil Woosnam who caused me problems and then Terry Paine at Southampton was a good player as well. He could beat you on either side, but he'd also got a bit of devil in him and he could go over the top if you didn't watch it. Southampton wanted to sign me after one game down there when I'd finally managed to keep Paine quiet. They bid £10,000 Waddo later told me, but the board turned it down. I wouldn't have gone anyway as I didn't want to leave.

At St James' Park, it went from bad to worse then as Newcastle got a third before half-time when my clearance was headed back into the box and Hilley went round Jimmy to put them 3-2 up. We couldn't believe it and it shocked us a bit. There was no way back as Newcastle scored twice more in the second half, one after Jimmy failed to hold on to a shot and they netted the rebound and one a storming free-kick in the last minute just to really rub it in.

I think we carried that into the next game against Scunthorpe a bit. We were still missing Stan and Dennis, so we didn't have our first choice attack out. Add to that young John Ritchie, who had deputised for Dennis, was also injured up at Newcastle, so youngster Keith Bebbington filled in for Stan on the wing and Eddie Clamp had to play in attack as an emergency inside-forward. Former England international though he was, Clampy would be the first to have told you that his strength wasn't being creative. He was a destroyer – in more ways than one.

Again against Scunthorpe we scored first when Ratter nipped in to lash a rebound from an Asprey shot into the roof of the net. But then Scunthorpe scored twice in a couple of minutes, I remember one being a fantastic header by a striker called McGuigan. They outplayed us really and we only got back into the game thanks to a spectacularly lucky goal. Eddie Stuart just belted the ball forward from wide out on the right and it sailed over the keeper and into the net. We thought we'd got away with it then, but Scunthorpe scored with another header in the last few minutes. Then Clampy missed an open goal when he didn't quite connect properly with a volley and it just wasn't our day.

I really remember how the crowd that day went from cheering us on at the start, to total silence by the end. It was eerie. Things had been going so well, but the three defeats since the incredible night against Madrid had everyone biting their fingernails.

BUT ALL THAT meant was that we had a fantastic climax to the season with the trip to Chelsea assuming huge importance. It was a vital, vital game. Remember Stoke hadn't won promotion for 30-odd years. Most people couldn't even remember it. And it had been ten years since they'd played in the top flight. Before Stan came, crowds were around the 6-8,000 mark. The club had been in dire straits, but now we were on the verge of some success.

Promotion fever was everywhere around the city. I remember one group of Stoke fans from Biddulph painted this vintage car in red and white stripes and drove down to watch the game. I later found out that it was a 1930 Austin 12 and eight supporters had clubbed together to buy it towards the end of that promotion season, so they could travel about to games, including down to the Vic, in this beautifully painted striped car!

Those three defeats had brought us back into the chasing pack, which was now down to two clubs, Chelsea and Sunderland. We had 49 points and four games to play, Chelsea 48 points and three games left, and Sunderland 48 points and three remaining matches. The good news for us was that the other two still had to meet each other at Sunderland, so we knew someone would drop points there. Ultimately, of course, with only two clubs going up in those days, one of us would miss out.

The great news was that Stan and Dennis were both fit for Chelsea. Our side was at full strength. The week before the game, Stan had been named as Footballer of the Year. That was a red rag to a bull as far as Ron Harris was concerned. He was a young whipper-snapper back then, full of cockney mouth and he publicly declared that he would sort Matthews out. He was beginning to style himself as the 'Chopper' although I don't think the nickname was widely in use at that stage, as he'd only played a few games.

He spent the first few minutes of the match trying to kick Stan as hard as he could. Stan hurdled the challenges and avoided most of the kicks, but then Harris connected viciously. But that was when Eddie Clamp came into his own. Clampy was a very hard man on the football pitch. I was scared of him and he was on my side!

Apparently Eddie and Ron had had their differences during a game when Eddie was at Wolves the season before, so they knew each other well. After Harris had fouled Stan, Clampy goes over to him and says, "You leave him alone or you'll have me to answer to." And he did leave Stan alone after that, although mainly because he didn't get near him!

All Stan did was rub the back of his leg where Harris had kicked him very slowly. He didn't say a word, but I could see there was a look of determination in his eyes. After that he gave Harris such a chasing. Ron couldn't get near him. It was magic.

Harris just wanted to kick Matthews. He'd said so in the papers beforehand, so we knew what he was up to. He was young then and wanted to make a name for himself, but it ended up with his own crowd booing him. They didn't like it at all. They'd actually come to see Matthews play as much as see Chelsea win. You wouldn't get that these days, and it shows you how Matthews had captured people's imagination during his career. Even at 48, people wanted to see him play. He had that sort of presence and that aura about him after everything he'd done in his career.

Chelsea had actually started the game well, having most of the early attacks and Jimmy O'Neill made a couple of good saves. I remember after one of them I ran over to him and picked him off the floor and shouted at him, "That's what I want!" In those previous three games he'd had a few dodgy moments, so I wanted to let him know that he was doing what he did best again.

Waddo had us set up to play it tight and look to score on the break. A classic away tactic, I suppose. It worked and we frustrated Chelsea. I had to mark Murray and thought I did a pretty decent job of keeping him quiet. In fact I don't think I really gave him a kick. But we had a brief to get forward when we could as it was important to try to win the game. Two points would be great for us, but ensuring Chelsea also got none would do wonders for our promotion hopes. So I picked this ball up about 40 yards out, ran on a bit and then thought I'd have a crack. I caught it beautifully and it fizzed towards the top corner. But Bonetti was in goal for Chelsea and he just got his hand to it to keep it out.

Mainly we just kept trying to work the ball out to Stan who was tormenting Harris constantly, leaving him on the ground as he tried to make more and more desperate challenges. I remember there is a fantastic picture of Stan in that match. He's running towards the camera with both Ron Harris and Eddie McCreadie lying strewn on the ground having missed their tackles as Stan swerved past them. He really did take them totally to the cleaners.

It was from one of these attacks that we did finally score. Matthews passed to Jackie Mudie, who nudged it on to Jimmy McIlroy, arriving on the edge of the penalty area with immaculate timing. He drove the ball right-footed across Bonetti and in off the far post. It was a really well-worked goal and it hit Chelsea hard, coming about ten minutes before the break.

Skill was definitely winning this battle and Viollet, Mudie and McIlroy were at the hub of everything, bringing Stan and Ratter into play on the wings whenever they could. We defended well too, and rode our luck. Murray hit one shot inches wide and then failed to control the ball from a cross and I nipped in to clear it. If he'd killed it and shot first time I don't think I'd have got to that one, and it may have beaten Jimmy O'Neill, but fortunately he didn't. Then Bridges cracked a shot which hit the angle of post and bar and bounced away to safety. But that was the last chance Chelsea had. We held on comfortably in the end.

It was the best performance as a football team that I ever played in. It was a brilliant performance, absolutely brilliant. We deserved to win. And they had a good side out I tell you. Bobby Tambling was a cracking inside-forward. He went on to become Chelsea's all-time goalscorer. I think he still is actually. The winger that I marked, Murray, was a tricky player too. Recently I went over to Peterborough to see a game and went into a pub for a pre-match drink and there behind the bar running the pub was this same guy, Murray. Small world in't it?!

They were the side that at the start of the season, if you'd put money on anyone going up, it would have been them. They'd only been relegated the season before and had a good blend of experience from the team which had won the title a few years earlier and a fantastic youth team, who'd already produced the likes of Jimmy Greaves and later Peter Osgood and Alan Hudson. One product of that set-up was Terry Venables, who was a good midfielder. He played at every level for England – I believe he is the only player ever to go through all the ranks and win a cap at every single level. He was a quality footballer, but he was a bit cocky even then!

THE FINAL WHISTLE sounded and we knew we'd pulled off a fantastic result, one which put us right in control of our destiny and that was what we had wanted. Better still it hurt Chelsea, one of our nearest rivals. One of the biggest aspects of that day was the crowd at Stamford Bridge. It was an unbelievable gate of over 66,000. That was the biggest in London outside Wembley all season – and for a Second Division match too. I don't know if it's ever been beaten for a Second Division game, but I loved the atmosphere. It was extremely special, and made all the more so because there were thousands of Stoke fans there, who'd travelled down to cheer us on. It wasn't so easy to travel around in those days and we really appreciated those fans turning up to support us. It does help, particularly in big away games, when fans make themselves heard. Stamford Bridge back then wasn't like it is today. It had a dog track around it, so the stands were a long way from the pitch. Then there was the Shed end as they call it now. In my day it was called the Cowshed! That's what it looked like, this big barn roof over a huge curved terrace. We defended that end in the second half and I remember looking up at it and seeing this huge sea of faces. It was an incredible sight. Of course, they pretty much all went home disappointed!

We now knew we just needed one more win to guarantee promotion. But to top it all off we went to Bury three days later and lost! Thankfully we clinched it by beating Luton at home on the following Saturday. We had a promotion party at a hotel in Newcastle near the hospital. It was where we had all our parties, especially the Christmas ones. They were great nights.

DON'T GET ME wrong, playing for England was absolutely brilliant, and something I never thought I'd ever, ever do. Some people would say playing for England was better than a club promotion, but this performance was the best in probably the most important game that I ever played in and it meant everything to us to set up that promotion.

JIMMY O'NEILL: BORN 13 OCTOBER 1931, DUBLIN; 149 GAMES, 0 GOALS

Jimmy O'Neill

Stoke City 2 Luton Town 0

League Division Two

Saturday 18 May 1963

I WAS THE first player Tony Waddington ever signed, but I never really wanted to join Stoke. I was devastated when I left Everton and I definitely didn't want to leave the club. Johnny Carey was the Everton manager then. I'd been first choice for five years, but he preferred this other goalkeeper called Dunlop. But I didn't think he was much of a keeper and I had a row with Carey over it. I was only 29 and I had plenty of years left in me. As a matter of fact I had some great seasons at Stoke and played as well as I had at Everton.

Liverpool were supposed to be interested in signing me and if I had got an offer from them I would have joined as it would have meant not moving house, even though it would have meant playing for the red half of the city. I wasn't that keen on moving to Stoke initially. I really hated the Victoria Ground as a visiting player. I remember we won 4-2 with Everton the season we won promotion, 1953/54, my first season in the first team. I thought it was a rubbish ground; there were no decent baths in the old main stand for away teams. But I suppose that was what was good about the Vic for Stoke, opponents were intimidated by it, there was a great atmosphere and noise and teams hated going there. I certainly appreciated it more once I'd signed for the club!

Liverpool were supposed to be interested and if I had got an offer from them I would have joined as it would have meant not moving house, even though it would have meant playing for the red half of the city.

I WAS THE baby of a family of five; three sisters and a brother. We were all still living at home, but then my father died when I was 16. And I don't think he would have let me go over the water to England if he'd still been alive because I was the baby of the family.

I was spotted playing in a youth international at Brentford. I was playing for the Republic of Ireland and we beat England 1-0. Everton asked me to come over for a month's trial, and the manager, Cliff Britton it was then, said he wasn't sure about me, but he'd give me another month's trial. At the end of that he said that he'd give me a year's contract, but I'd have to prove that I was better than the six other goalkeepers they'd got on their books if he was to keep me on after that. That kind of motivated me!

I did OK and he kept me on and I improved during each of the next few seasons. Then I played in a friendly in the pre-season of 1953/54, it was the first time I'd ever been away with the first team, and I think I impressed the manager enough for him to make me the first choice goalkeeper. We won promotion that season, back to the First Division, after the club had been relegated three years previously, and Everton has never been relegated since, which is an incredible record. Only Arsenal has been in the top flight longer. We established the club back in the First Division and I became the regular goalkeeper and playing for Ireland.

I won my first cap in 1952, although it didn't go so well. We got beat 6-0 by Spain! In fact we were 2-0 down before I actually touched the ball in play. The first two occasions I touched it was picking it out of the back of the net. The funny thing was I retained my place for the next match and got Player of the Month in the Irish press. I played 17 times for my country and loved every minute, although we weren't the strongest team. We did have some good results though. We beat the Wunderteam of Austria 4-0, which was a fantastic result.

I never played in an international match whilst at Stoke, although I did get a cap! There was a player called John O'Neill who played for Preston and the Irish FA sent me his cap. He only won one and they sent it to me by mistake! I had to send it back, of course, but there's Irish administration for you.

My strong point as a goalkeeper was my shot-stopping and my aerial work. I was very good in the air, very good. I could come out into a crowded penalty area and collect crosses above players, even though I was only 5ft 10in. No trouble. I was pretty springy in the legs, which made me good in the air, jumping for these high balls. They always say that you should take the ball at its highest point and I was able to do that very well.

I was always a heavy smoker, even at Everton; 40 or 50 a day. I used to smoke before games and at half-time too. At Stoke I'd be in the toilet before the game for a cigarette and then hide my fags in my trouser pocket and finish it off at half-time. It helped calm my nerves and I don't think Tony Waddington knew anything about it.

Everyone had nerves. Quite a few used to get sick before a game, including Stan Matthews. A lot of players smoked in those days. We didn't know what we know now about smoking.

We had some fun in training at Stoke. I remember taking on Don Ratcliffe in a sprint after one training session. It was a challenge race. He thought he was the fastest at the club, but I was off, ahead of him, right from the start. I got ahead after 20 yards and turned round to egg him on! I beat him. He didn't appreciate that much!

I WAS THE first of the 'Old Crocks' to sign for the club. Tony had seen how the experienced Dennis Wilshaw had brought on the younger players in the side, and decided to blend the kids with more experience. It was a good policy. Stoke had been only getting a few thousand in 1961/62, but as soon as Stan came back it just took off. Mudie and Viollet were added to the mix and we all lifted our games and played very well in that promotion season.

I always have a good word for Tony Waddington. He was a clever man, make no mistake. He was a good man too. He brought players on, you know; Allen, Skeels and Ratcliffe. He brought them on and blended them with the more experienced players. He was good at making you feel that bit special. Although having said that he didn't have to say too much because he couldn't tell me how to play in goal and you couldn't tell Matthews how to play on the wing.

He always treated me reasonably well. However, I was disappointed to lose my place early in the following season up in Division One to a goalkeeper I didn't think was any better than me, Bobby Irvine. Then Lawrie Leslie came in and I didn't rate him that much either. I was better than both of them. Waddo told me that he thought I should move on. He wanted younger goalkeepers, but age doesn't matter so much to keepers. I was third choice then and so not playing on a Saturday. I was only 33 and I needed to play football, so I went to Darlington for a year and then to play for the Vale for a few seasons.

I PLAYED ALL 42 league games in one hell of a season when we won promotion in 1962/63. The Chelsea game was a huge game and we won 1-0, Ron Harris was humiliated by Stan Matthews and Jimmy McIlroy scored the winning goal that day after a bit of passing between him and Stan and Jackie Mudie. It was a good goal. It was some game, a very big game – and what a crowd, 66,000. Chelsea eventually finished runners-up, so it was very important that we beat them. We now needed just one more win to clinch the title and with it promotion.

That winter had been unbelievable. Unbelievable. We were up to our eyes in snow and sludge. The grounds were unplayable. Some of the other teams did manage to play the odd game, but they lost and so we ended up coming out of it still ahead, but now with three or four games in hand. Then we were playing twice a week of course, playing catch up with the fixtures, and the season was extended by a couple of week, so it didn't finish until late May.

I remember the third round FA Cup tie at Leeds, which didn't take place until early March. It was strange because we actually didn't want to win that cup tie. The competition had progressed enough that the next two rounds had been drawn and we'd be away in both if we got through. That meant more tough games and our focus was on winning promotion. So we really didn't want to win, but we found ourselves 1-0 ahead at half-time. I've never had any other game in which we were ahead that I didn't want to win! I actually wanted Leeds to score and they did. I'm not saying we deliberately lost that game, or I deliberately let two goals in, but I was relieved that we did lose – although I loved the FA Cup and was disappointed with the whole situation. We even got congratulated by the chairman for losing. He said to me afterwards, "I'm glad you let that second one in." It was bizarre.

That game was on a Wednesday, and then our next league match was away at Norwich. We were now free to concentrate on the league having lost in the cup and, what's more, we then signed the wonderful Jimmy McIlroy, a fabulous inside-forward from Burnley, who'd been one of the best teams of the early 1960s and were sitting third in the top flight when he joined us. So it was Jimmy's debut at Carrow Road, and what happened? We got hammered 6-0! Every time Norwich came down the pitch they just scored. Everything went in, no matter what I or the defence did. I remember Stan shouting, "Give me the ball. Give me the ball." But I was thinking, we need to score by playing down the middle, not by giving it out to him." Heaven only knows what Jimmy must have been thinking! He was probably wondering, 'What have I done here?!'

But then we went on a fantastic run, winning the next six games and altogether eight out of the next ten. That put us on the brink of promotion.

THE VICTORIA GROUND pitch was about the worst I ever saw it. The winter had destroyed the grass. We didn't really see any for the remainder of the season. I remember the Stoke-on-Trent Boys team reached the final of the English Schools Trophy. They had a good side with the likes of Jackie Marsh and Denis Smith amongst them, who would later go on to have great careers at Stoke. The FA wanted the second leg of the final against Bristol played at the Vic on the evening after the Luton match, but the pitch just couldn't sustain that kind of use – well certainly not after a bizarre combination of sheep and Tony Waddington had finished with it!

Yes, sheep. Part of the reason the pitch was so bad was because, for some reason, the chairman allowed some sheep on to the pitch to graze. The grass needed cutting, so they let these sheep on to eat it. But they gobbled the lot. There wasn't a blade of grass left. I have no idea why he allowed it. Waddington went berserk over it, and chased the sheep off the pitch!

The other reason the pitch wasn't so good was that Stan loved it muddy. It gave him an advantage as he seemed to just be able to glide over the mud, while defenders wallowed in it. So Waddo used to water the pitch. He'd have the fire engines down there on a Saturday morning to splash gallons of water on to it and the bizarre thing was for that game against Luton, no one seemed to notice that the pitch was a quagmire despite the fact it was late May and a beautiful dry, sunny day!

IN THE END the boys team played in the midweek prior to the Luton game and dug the pitch up some more for us, but they won 5-1 on aggregate to retain the trophy, a fantastic achievement.

That same night we played at Gigg Lane, Bury knowing that if we won the match we would win promotion and the Second Division Championship. We'd won that great match at Chelsea, so what could go wrong? But then our talisman, Stan Matthews, picked up an injury after being kicked black and blue by Ron Harris. Our squad was quite thin on the ground by that stage due to a clutch of injuries, so Waddo brought in teenager Alan Philpott for his debut. It was a surprise choice as Alan was really a defender not an attacker.

The previous night Sunderland had won their penultimate game to go one point ahead of us on 52 points. But we knew that their last match was against Chelsea, which was a tough, tough fixture. More importantly, it meant at least one of them would drop points, if not both and gave us confidence that we knew a win was all that was required.

Thousands of fans travelled to Bury expecting us to clinch promotion, but it was a tense, rugged match. I remember having to make more saves than I was normally comfortable with. But then we scored a goal that should have settled our nerves and seen us on our way. After about 25 minutes Jackie Mudie finished off a rebound after their keeper had parried Viollet's shot. Jackie didn't hit it that well, but I remember watching as the ball went through a tangle of players and dribbled over the line into the corner of the net. That was a great feeling. Only an hour to hold out and we'd be there.

But in the way of things, Bury got the luckiest equaliser you'll ever see. It was a bit like the goal we'd conceded against Newcastle when Tony Allen and I got in a tangle, but this time Eddie Clamp's clearance hit the Bury forward Jones in the chest and bounced over my head and into the goal. I couldn't believe it. That was just before half-time and we really didn't need it.

Then two minutes after the restart, they got another lucky goal. Three times the winger Bartley shot and three times the ball was blocked by one of my defenders, but the last time he'd learnt. Instead of hitting a hit low drive towards goal, which we were all expecting, he chipped the ball up and over us all. It went right into the top corner. It was in fact a great goal, but I didn't think so at the time!

That defeat was tremendously disappointing, but the good thing was we had a chance to put it all right just three days later at home to relegation threatened Luton.

I remember the *Sentinel* headline the night before the game said, "Stan returns, Stoke should win promotion"! Talk about putting pressure on us, in fact on one man. But no one need have worried, Stan produced a moment of magic that lifted the supporters of their feet and on to cloud nine, so it did.

Stan was a good friend of mine and he'd often come the night before a game from Blackpool where he lived and visit me in my house at Pilkington Street in Stoke. Then we'd go out to the pictures on the Friday night to relax before the game.

We did need to relax on this occasion, because I think the Bury game had got to us a bit. Mind you, people forget that this game was a vital one for Luton too. They needed to win to stand any chance of staying up. They had some good players too. Ron Baynham, Jardine and Turner.

STAN WAS REALLY buzzing around that day. He used to come back to the penalty area and collect the ball from me. But I didn't really like to give it to him, because he'd always have a full-back closely marking him, so I was a bit worried he'd lose the ball.

But that day he turned on another magnificent performance, he had players sliding slightly to unbalance them and he'd be past them. He had incredible balance. Luton didn't know what was going on. Remember it was the middle of May, and they came up with moulded studs on expecting the pitch to be bone dry. In those days you didn't often go out on to the pitch beforehand, so Luton came out just before the game with their mouldeds on and quickly realised what a quagmire it was and they all had to go back off to change their boots!

WE HAD A lucky escape early on when their left winger Jardine got away and crossed right in front of me, but their centre-forward couldn't quite reach it, thankfully. I remember how pent up the tension felt in the crowd. The supporters were desperate for us to win, to achieve promotion in front of them that day, and you could cut the atmosphere with a knife. That transmitted itself to the players, I think, as the game was played at a slow pace and with a lot of mistakes. The mud didn't help of course!

It was obvious that a flash of inspiration was needed and we had enough quality within our team to provide it. Jackie Mudie had already gone close from one goalmouth scramble, but his shot had been beaten away. When the same thing happened a couple of minutes later, he remained composed and managed to drill the ball past the defenders on the line. I was at the other end, so I couldn't really see what was going on in all the melée. All I knew was that the ball hit the net and we were one up!

We got through to half-time unscathed, without too many problems actually. In fact we should have had a nerve-settling second, but Jackie snatched at a better chance than the one he'd scored when Dennis Viollet set him up and he skied the ball over the top.

But we couldn't have started the second half any better.

Luton pressed forward straight from the kick-off as they needed to score quickly, but the attack got broken up and the ball fell to Jimmy McIlroy to start a counter-attack. Out of the corner of his eye he spotted one Stanley Matthews haring through the middle of the field, over the mud and puddles as if he was 17 again. Stan still had a fair turn of speed and he used it on this occasion. Jimmy found the perfect through ball for Stan to run on to just inside the Luton half and then what happened next was pure poetry in motion. Stan raced through the middle with the ball glued to his right foot and about six Luton players all chasing him. He dropped his shoulder so the keeper went down on the edge of the area and then waltzed round him to the left to slide the ball into the net at the Boothen End. It was a truly great goal.

To say the crowd went berserk is an understatement. Delirious, crazy, you name it. The noise was immense. And the release of emotion was incredible too. We knew that was it. And what more fitting a player to score the goal that returned Stoke to the top flight than Stan?

We didn't really celebrate goals in those days – not like they do today with the choreographed routines and all that malarkey - but Stan was fair mobbed by the lads as he made his way back to the half-way line. Stan was such a cool character that he didn't show much emotion on the pitch either, but you could see how exhilarated he was by that goal.

We still had almost a half of the match to play, of course, but it was to all intents and purposes over. Luton knew they would not score three and we pretty much played out time as they got used to the idea of being relegated.

We then heard that Sunderland had been beaten at home 1-0 by Chelsea and that meant we were promoted, as champions! The crowd spilled on to the pitch and mobbed us all. I can't remember what happened then. It's all a blur after all these years, but it was wonderful. We eventually managed to get back into the dressing rooms, with the help of some policemen I think, and then were brought up into the new stand to wave our thanks to the thousands of people who were now on the pitch. They were chanting, "We Want Stan!" And quite right too. His goal was the icing on a special cake for everyone at the club, but especially the supporters who had seen the club almost dead on its knees before Stan's return in 1961. It was a very special moment.

We got a medal for winning the title, which I cherished. We had a dinner and there were lots of events to attend around the city, including a reception at the Lord Mayor's chambers, which I remember very well.

If you ever want to relive that incredible day then there is a film which was made by *World In Action*, who were following Stan for a documentary at the time and so captured the match and celebrations. Snippets of it are on the Video History of Stoke City, which I watch from time to time to remind me of the old days. They were truly wonderful.

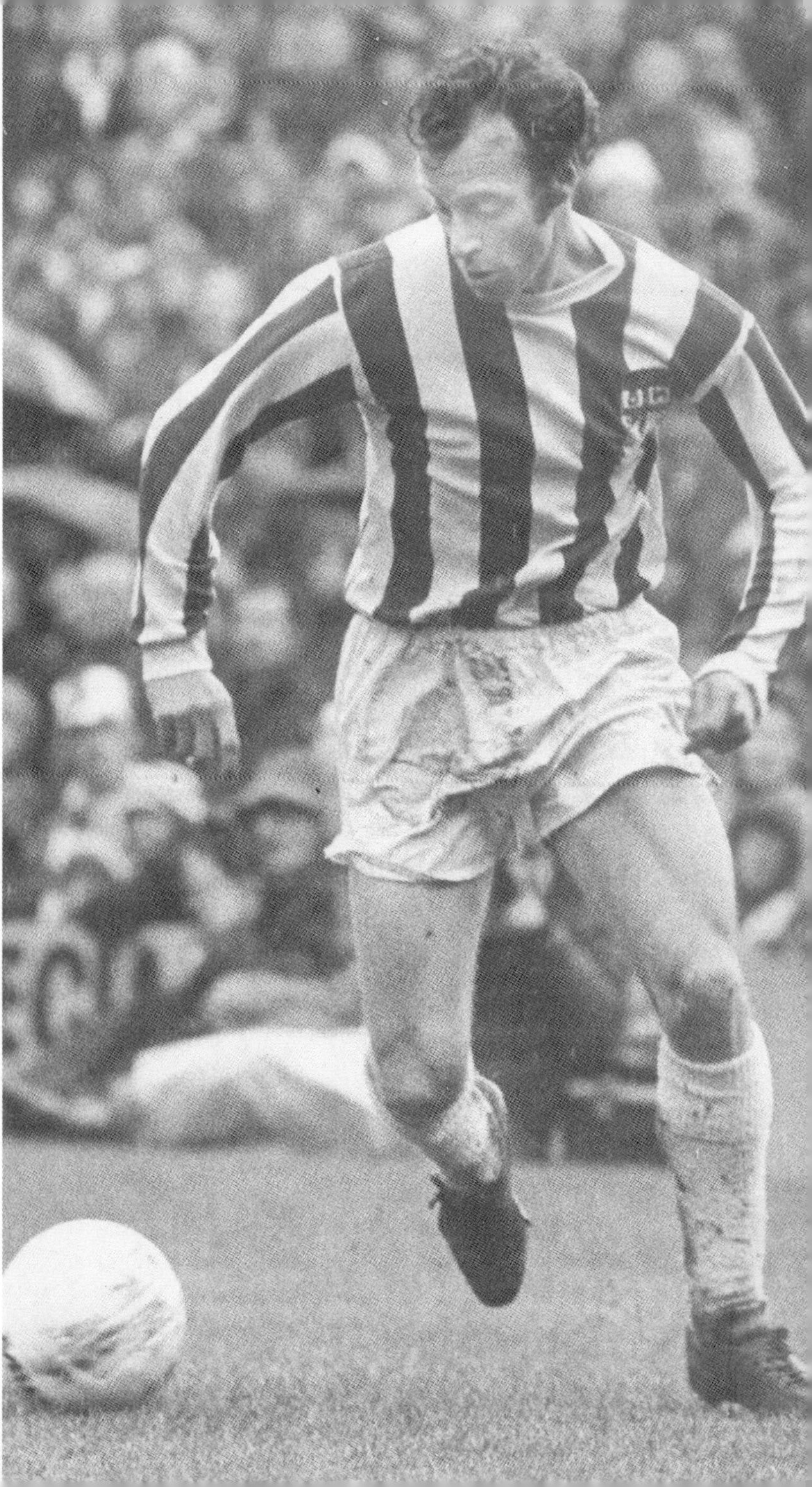

HARRY BURROWS: BORN 17 MARCH 1941, HAYDOCK; 284 GAMES, 76 GOALS

Harry Burrows

Stoke City 6 Aston Villa 1

League Division One

Saturday 10 December 1966

I MOVED TO Stoke for a fiver. Just £5. It's amazing when you think about it. Money really didn't matter back when I played. There wasn't a lot of difference between the wages you could earn at a club like Stoke and what you would be offered at Man United, Liverpool or Arsenal and that meant that good players were spread about a bit.

Having said that money was not quite as plentiful as it is these days, even in the Championship. What mattered more was if the club treated you right and Stoke were fantastic to me.

What made a difference was that the maximum wage, which had kept a lid on players' wages since time began, had just been lifted by George Eastham's court case against Newcastle, who had refused to release him from his contract when he wanted to move to Arsenal. It meant we could now negotiate our own contracts. The ceiling had been £20, but when it was lifted the England captain Johnny Haynes immediately became the first £100 a week player; a pay rise of 500 per cent! Clubs weren't paying silly money, but players were able to negotiate what they were worth.

That's what led me to join Stoke on a matter of principle.

I STARTED ON the groundstaff at Villa Park in 1957 after being spotted playing youth football in the Merseyside area and had eight great years there, so I loved Villa. They were a club close to my heart. I got into the first team in 1959, replacing the injured Peter McParland, a legendary Villa left winger who had scored both goals in their 1957 FA Cup final victory over Manchester United. We won promotion that season at the first attempt and went on to establish ourselves as a force back in the First Division. We got to the semi-finals of the FA Cup two years running as well, but lost 1-0 on both occasions to Nottingham Forest and Wolves, who both went on to win the final.

In the newly created League Cup we did well too, winning the first ever final. The competition wasn't exactly highly thought of to start with, and I suppose it still isn't taken hugely seriously. But not all the First Division clubs entered in the first few seasons. So we reached the final and it turned out to be against Rotherham United, who were then a lower table Second Division side. The final wasn't played at Wembley for the first few seasons of the competition's existence, it was a two-legged affair played at the start of the following 1961/62 season because of fixture congestion. We actually lost the first leg at Millmoor 2-0, but turned it around in the second leg at home, which was a great night. I scored the second goal as we won 3-0 to become the first ever winners of the League Cup.

We again got to the final in 1963, but lost to Birmingham City 3-1 on aggregate. We had a very good side at Villa under Joe Mercer, the manager. He encouraged us to play expansive football. But when he left in the summer of 1964 it all started to go wrong.

At the start of the 1964/65 season I asked for what I thought was a fairly modest rise. I'd been there for eight years, had played for the England under-23s, scored 73 goals in 181 games, not bad for a left-winger, finished as leading scorer twice and I'd just got married. I was happy to negotiate my own wages. I've always thought that you should be able to stand up for yourself. I could never have used an agent. I don't think they're needed actually. If you've got any brains or sense you should be able to negotiate your own contract. I would have hated to be manipulated by an agent as some players are now. It can damage your career. I was happy to earn what I thought I was worth and stay loyal. I feel sorry for managers now and I never thought I'd say that!

I knew that Villa were signing new players on better pay than what those of us who were already at the club were getting. I don't think they appreciated how that made us feel. Remember this was situation was new for all of us. Anyway I went in to see the new manager, Dick Taylor, and I only asked for a £5 pay rise and I thought I deserved that. But it was refused, so in those days you could go on to a monthly rolling contract, so I refused to sign a new two season deal in the summer of 1965, went on the monthly contract and put my name on the transfer list at Christmas.

I thought it was backward thinking for Villa. I wasn't asking for the earth and I'd done the business for eight years and just wanted parity with these new signings. I was quite prepared to sign if they'd given me the £5 a week straight away as I liked it there, and I wouldn't have listened to any other offers whatever another club was paying.

Suddenly the club woke up to what was going on and they offered me the rise I'd asked for and also offered to backdate all my pay to the beginning of the season. By now it was coming up to March time and transfer deadline day was looming. I really didn't want to leave, but it all came about on a matter of principle really over my pay. I did not like the way they had gone about things and I was my own man, so I refused their offer and waited for clubs to come in for me.

It was silly really. A lot of the team had all come into the side together and we were all good friends, so it was ridiculous that they were ignoring us in favour of these new signings, who weren't as good

So in the end Tony Waddington enquired about me on transfer deadline day. I had a call to say that I should go up to Stoke, so I did and the terms I was offered were great - £15 a week more, which was quite a lot in those days. The club were signing decent players at the time. Waddington had brought in George Eastham, Peter Dobing, Calvin Palmer, George Kinnell and Maurice Setters since they'd got promoted. The press were saying that the club were only signing older players. Well, as I'd signed on my 24th birthday I thought that made me a veteran straight away! Peter Dobing was only 25 and played for another eight years, so he wasn't exactly past it either!!

The club seemed to be going places and I would be able to travel from my home in Birmingham to Stoke without me moving to start off with. So I signed. And to show you how Tony Waddington made you feel wanted, after I'd played a few games and done very well - scoring on my debut was a good start - Waddo called me into his office and ripped up my contract in front of me. I couldn't believe it. I didn't understand what was going on. Then he said, "Harry you've done so well I'm going to give you another fiver a week." I couldn't believe it. The difference between how he treated me and how the Villa had was incredible. That made me feel wanted and despite the status which came with playing for a club like Villa, who were considered one of the very biggest clubs then, I settled in to Stoke well and really enjoyed my time there.

To show you what a folly the Villa's wage policy was they lost a lot of players around then including the likes of Tony Hateley, and went on to get relegated just after that (1966/67) and then went down to the Third Division not long after (1969/70). It took a change of manager and a change of owner and even then until 1975 for them to get back up to the First Division again.

WE USED TO play some great football at Stoke. Tony Waddington got us fit and left us to it more or less. His skill was to bring good, experienced players in. Roy Vernon, a Welsh international inside-forward from Everton, arrived on the same day as me; deadline day 1965. He was a classy player. About 9st 7lb wet through. He liked a smoke did Roy, or Taffy as we used to call him. We used to joke that he could smoke in the shower! And he could. He'd always have a cigarette on the go, and would spark up straight after a game, keeping his cigarette out of the water while he showered.

Then two years later Gordon Banks arrived. We had a really good side and we played off-the-cuff football. John Ritchie was a great striker, still quite young like me, certainly not an 'Old Crock'! He scored lots of goals and could shoot with either foot and was great in the air. I notched plenty as well. I finished as top scorer in 1967/68 with 16 goals in all competitions. I really enjoyed playing in that side.

I'd started off my career as a kid as an inside-forward and it was Joe Mercer who had converted me to a left-winger. Teams played with two wingers then and my job was to take on the full-back, get to the byline and get a cross over. I enjoyed cutting in and shooting too. That was where most of my goals came from. I had a good shot in either foot, but my left foot had a great shot in it. I'd been nicknamed 'Blast' at Villa, but Stoke fans called me 'Cannonball' because of my left foot shot.

Football was a natural thing for me. As a kid I just played on the park and in the street. There were two huge things which changed football for the worse during my time that I think we're still suffering from today. Tactically I think that the England World Cup victory in 1966 was quite detrimental to the way football has gone since then. Suddenly wingers were out of fashion and sides played with four across the midfield, keeping it tight. That was all down to Alf Ramsey playing with no wingers. I don't think it was to the benefit of football, although it won England the World Cup. It was a backward step in a lot of respects, the long ball game came in and in my opinion it destroyed football. It wasn't worth watching if you ask me. Wimbledon would bang it straight up front, missing out the midfield and the game was all based on a player's size, not their ability. You'd hear coaches asking, "Is he big enough?" Not, "Can he play?"

Then there was the FA coaching course which was run by this guy called Charlie Hughes. He thought he could create footballers. His blueprint was someone who was 6ft 6in and could run all day. What a load of rubbish. At the end of the day it's a skill thing. It's about ability. I remember at the tail end of my career when I went to Plymouth I saw one coach telling a youth team player where to put his foot to kick the ball. Well, he'd obviously got no chance of making it if he'd got to sixteen and wasn't able to kick properly! He must have got there because he could run all day. That's no good. If you can't kick a ball at sixteen you really might as well give up.

If you've got players of ability you've always got a chance. But you need a mix to have a balanced team. I was lucky to be at Stoke as Waddo liked football being played and he'd assembled a team of ball players who could attack. We weren't as restricted as they are today. We could be creative in that last third of the pitch. We attacked as a team and played with width, which is something I believe in. Even today the top sides have width; United have Ronaldo, Chelsea have Robben. You notice it when they don't play. It does affect the balance of those teams. These days often you see all the players crowded into a small area of the pitch at lower levels as they are all trying to reduce risk and stop mistakes. It kills the game if you ask me. They play the percentages and it can get quite boring.

I remember at Plymouth we had a coach with a clipboard, who had one corner kick that he wanted us to take. We practised it over and over again. But it was predictable and I remember this one match when I took several of these corners and nothing was happening, so the next corner I tried something different and he shouted at me, "What do you think you're doing?"

And I replied, "Well, it wasn't working, so I tried something else."

"No," he says. "This is the way we do it and you keep to that." Ridiculous.

I SUPPOSE I was quite quick and fairly good on the ball in terms of dribbling and in those days you would only have the full-back against you. Nowadays it is harder to get behind the full-back because they double mark attackers because they bring the wide midfielder back. Getting past them and down to the byline was what we used to work on because you can play nice today football in front of the full-back all day long, but it wouldn't worry them. If you get past them, however, and get them turned and chasing after you, then they'd have problems. So the idea from us was to get behind them and create havoc that way. I sometimes tried to dribble or beat my man for pace, and then other times I would play one-twos with my inside-forward, usually George Eastham. I could hardly head a ball, but that wasn't my job. I was there to provide opportunities.

There were a lot of good full-backs around in those days. Jimmy Armfield at Blackpool was the England right-back, but I always seemed to do well against him. I scored a hat-trick for Villa against him up at Bloomfield Road. He wasn't a tough-tackling full-back, he was classy, a ball player. Paul Reaney at Leeds was a tough customer, then Roger Byrne at Liverpool was also a good, hard full-back. Of course tackling from behind was allowed then, so you had to learn to look after yourself. You knew that early on, with their first tackle, those hard full-backs would try to put you in the stand. Even if they hurt you, though, you couldn't let them know, as once they knew that, they'd got the mettle on you. They'd have you for toast then.

We had quite a small team actually. Eric Skeels was quite small, he was like a Nobby Stiles type of player; a terrier. His job was to win the ball and give it to the creative players. He didn't have the glamour job, but you need players like that to get a good balance in the side. Tony Allen was a classy player. He could run with the ball as well as any forward. He was a footballing full-back. Then there was right-half Calvin Palmer. He was a good wholehearted player who had a lot of skill as well. In fact the whole team could use the ball. The likes of Dennis Viollet, Peter Dobing and Jimmy McIlroy were renowned names with experience, who could really play football.

George Kinnell was a good, hard centre-half. He was just like Denis Smith. He would put his head in anywhere. Centre-halves have to have that bit of devilment and bite in them, although I think just to be a professional footballer you need a bit of that.

TONY WADDINGTON WAS quite forward thinking in some ways. We used to have athletes coming in to take us for pre-season running. We had a bloke named Hargreaves who was at Madeley College and was one of the early sports scientists. It was very modern thinking at the time. They even talked about diets even then. They gave us diet sheets, which told us to avoid smoking and drinking in excess. We enjoyed a drink of course, but we didn't really do anything to excess.

Our stamina training was done on Trentham hills. Tony Waddington was very clever. He got Roy Fowler, who lived at Leek and was the British cross-country champion, to come along and take us on long runs. Then once we'd got the stamina he'd get Derek Ibbotson, another local lad, the British three-mile champion to do track work. And then we had a sprinter come in as well to work us over short distances for speed training. That definitely got us fit and made a difference during games.

The club wasn't all quite so modern though. I remember on my debut at Wolves we travelled down to Molineux on a PMT bus. Although we'd got all these great players, we went PMT! And then Roy Vernon and I, who were both making our debuts having signed on deadline day, put our shirts on and they hung below our knees; neither of us were particularly big. So Roy got some scissors and cut the bottom few inches of his shirt off! We did gradually progress from that level, but at the time we wondered what we'd come to as we'd both been at very big clubs in Villa and Everton, where we had modern coaches to travel to games in and kit that fitted!

There was always a good atmosphere at the Victoria Ground. Being on the wing I had a good rapport with the crowd and I would meet the supporters in the café during the week having my lunch after training. Of course now they jump in their Jags or BMWs and tootle off. They don't mix with the crowd. For the first seven years of my career I didn't have a car and I used to travel on the bus to training. Being a footballer felt like a normal job and you were a normal person having your lunch with the workers.

Stan Matthews retired at the end of the 1964/65 season and we went on a post-season tour to Scandinavia and Russia. We played in Copenhagen and that was the last game he played for Stoke. He was 50 then. Incredible. It was the only time I played with him.

Back then Stoke were heavily in demand as a touring club because of Matthews. His name was a fantastic draw. He was the first global sporting superstar. Even after he left it meant that Stoke were asked to play high-profile overseas friendlies. Another game I remember was when we went to Barcelona to play and I scored the third goal as we went 3-0 ahead at half-time. They came back, but we hung on to win 3-2. I nearly chose that game as my favourite match, but after all it wasn't a competitive game.

BECAUSE OF ALL my time at Villa and what had gone on when I left the club, playing against them was always special to me. My second game for Stoke was actually against Villa and it felt very strange to be lining up against them. We won that game 2-1 at the Victoria Ground and then beat them home and away the following season, 1965/66, and I scored all three of the goals. We won 1-0 at Villa Park and 2-0 at home. So I'd really got the taste for beating my old club!

As I say, it was strange to be playing against them, but once I'd made the move I just got on with it. I have a soft spot for Villa and I still go back, but when I was playing for Stoke they were definitely my team and I wanted to win every game.

So the game I have chosen as my magic match was the clubs' first meeting the following season, in December 1966. Villa hadn't had the best of starts to the league season and were struggling, although they had just scored a shock win over Manchester United, but they were vulnerable away from home. Stoke had begun the season well and were fifth going into the match, although we'd been badly beaten at Leicester the previous weekend.

WE'D TAKEN THE lead at Filbert Street through my penalty. I liked taking pens. I used to hit them as hard as I could. That spot-kick was against Gordon Banks and I never gave him a hope! But we'd lost the game 4-2 and hadn't played very well at all despite that early lead.

The only change to that side for the Villa game was the return of first choice John Farmer in goal in place of Harry Gregg, the old Manchester United and Northern Ireland international. John played for England under-23s and was a tremendous goalkeeper. He was unlucky that Tony decided to sign the world's greatest goalkeeper in Gordon Banks in 1967.

George Eastham opened the scoring early on. It was actually his first goal for the club in his 21st game. He picked up the ball inside the area, drew a tackle and then slotted it home coolly with his left foot. He was such a classy player. He'd been in Alf Ramsey's World Cup squad, but didn't get a game because of the way Ramsey chose to play. We actually had a lot of good left-footed players in the squad. Myself, George and Peter Dobing were all naturally left-sided and funnily enough we all scored that day.

My direct full-back opponent was a guy named Bradley who had only just come into the Villa team. He'd been playing in the Central League when I was at the club. Villa still had some good players in Alan Deakin, Charlie Aitken, the other full-back, and John Sleeuwenheek. I'd played with John in the Villa youth team and he'd progressed to the England under-23s, but I didn't think their team was half as good as it had been before all the unrest and changes.

Given that we won 6-1 you'd have expected us to run away with it a bit, but Villa actually equalised and were in the game for a while. I can't really remember their goal; all that gets lost in the mists of time a bit. You only really remember the important ones you score yourself, let alone the goals that get scored against you. I always wanted to forget them!

But we cut loose a bit after that and I was fortunate enough to score a hat-trick. It was one of those games. I was motivated for any game, so it wasn't a major revenge mission or anything. The chances just fell perfectly for me. The strange thing was I hadn't scored that many goals that year. I'd only got a couple, including that penalty the week before, so I wasn't in any particular great scoring form.

My first came when I got the ball 25 yards out and tried a shot, which was blocked. But the ball came back to me and I shot again from outside the box. Fortunately the ball took a bit of a deflection, which took it right into the far corner of the goal. Then Roy Vernon laid me on a beautiful pass, which I cracked home from the edge of the area left-footed. Finally, after half-time, I scored a very rare headed goal for me, coming in at the far post from a Peter Dobing cross from the right. I think I was around about the penalty spot when I put my head on it.

That was in front of the Boothen End and I did my usual goal celebration which was to stand still and pretend to shoot cans. I didn't go mad when I scored, but I did like to do the shooting cans thing. The Boothen End was very influential and they had this guy called Zigger Zagger who was the instigator of the songs. The singing was great and of course it still goes on to this day.

I remember Peter Dobing was very influential that day. In fact he had scored our fourth goal straight after the restart with a beautifully judged lob from the edge of the box. That was a tremendous goal.

The sixth and final goal came from Roy Vernon, who played really well that day. I ran at the full-back and beat him on the inside and slipped a ball through for Taffy to run on to just inside the box. He cracked it home and we'd got six goals!

I don't think the Villa fans had a go at me for scoring so many times against them. I'd always had a good rapport with those supporters and they never gave me any gip, despite being one of their former players who always seemed to do well against them. They knew I hadn't just left for the sake of it, so they didn't boo me or anything.

I read the *Sentinel* match report recently to refresh my memory for doing this book and I found a really nice piece about me:

> 'Harry could not put a foot wrong. He finished with a hat-trick of goals which had the Victoria Ground aglow with anticipation every time he got possession. He produced the thrusting power which leavened the often brilliant pattern of weaving of his colleagues.'

The result left us fourth in the league and that hat-trick began a great run of scoring for me. I scored in four of the next six games and ended up scoring 17 goals that season, only finishing three behind John Ritchie as leading scorer.

To score that hat-trick, including one with my head even – which was very unusual - probably that's why I remember this game as much as any other. You don't often play in a team that scores six either. But Villa went down that season, so in another way it was a bit sad.

I go and watch games at both Stoke and Villa now. At both clubs us old players get looked after and we raise a lot of money for charity. I enjoy that side of things. All the players got on well at Stoke and it was a very homely club in those days. The Directors would always come along to dos and it was just like family. I couldn't fault it. I spoke to George Eastham recently and he told me that Stoke was the best club he played for and he'd been at both Arsenal and Newcastle. Everyone who played at that time looks back on it as their fondest memory. I know I do.

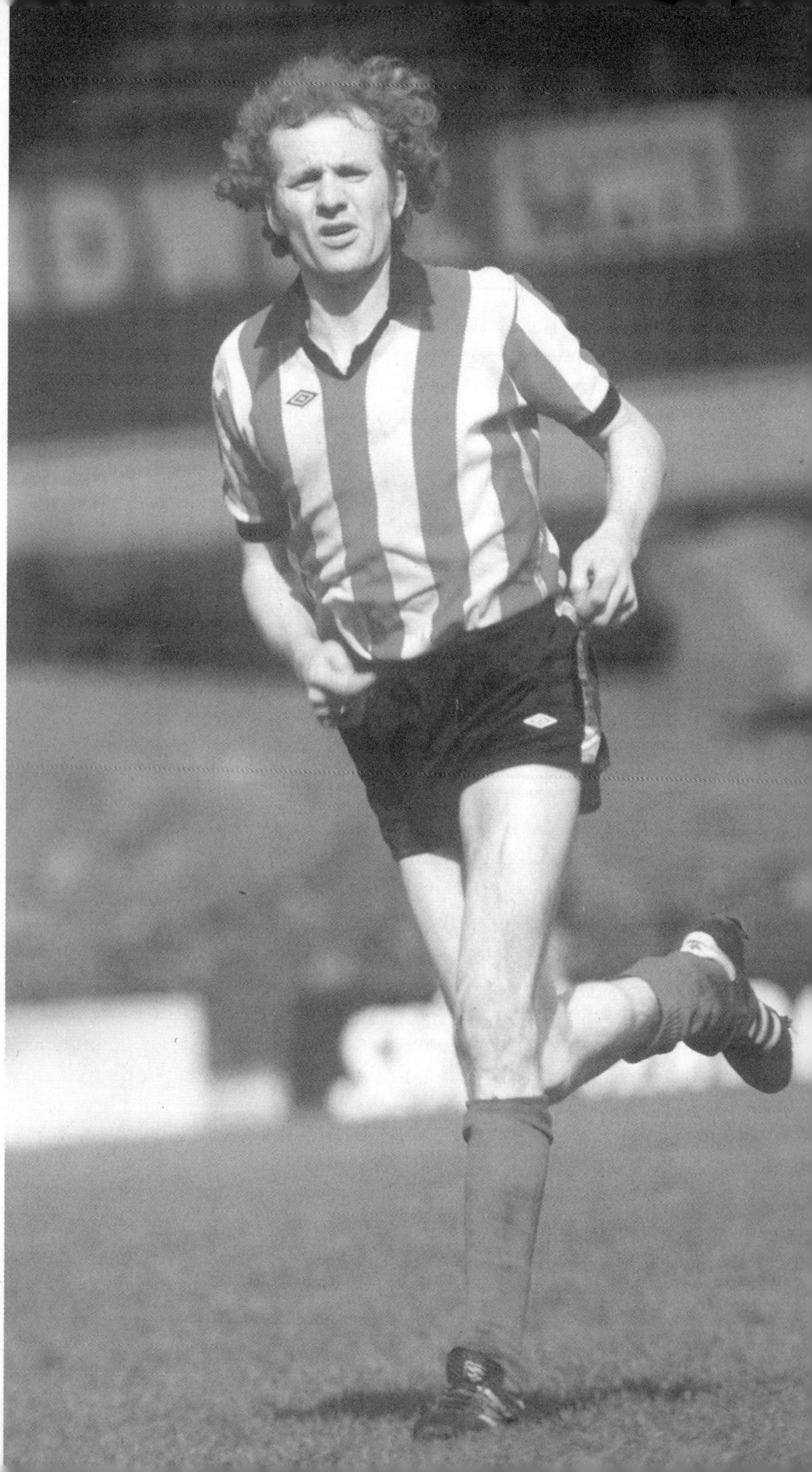

TERRY CONROY: BORN 2 OCTOBER 1946, DUBLIN; 297 GAMES, 103 GOALS

Terry Conroy

Chelsea 1 Stoke City 2

League Cup Final

Saturday 4 March 1972

THERE WAS A new scoreboard at Wembley and I was looking up at it. But there seemed to be some mistake. It had my name on it, 'Conroy 4'. I was dazed and confused by this eventuality and was constantly drawn to the words on the scoreboard. It was uncanny. I kept looking round to find the referee as I was sure he was going to disallow the goal, the goal I had just scored at Wembley. Yes, I had scored in a cup final at WEMBLEY!!! I didn't want to wake up.

It was as if the world had focussed in on me and I stood still while everything else kept on swirling around me; the noise of the fans celebrating wildly, some singing my name, the movement of the players continuing on with the game and then, in the midst of all that, I could hear someone calling my name:

"Terry, Terry. Fucking snap out of it."

Jackie Marsh grabbed me by the shoulders and shook me hard. He might only be little, Marshy, but he was strong and he rattled me good and proper. He'd had Waddo bending his ear to make me snap out of it and within a few seconds I'd suffered a hard tackle from a Chelsea opponent and I was back to earth again.

There's no room for passengers in a Wembley final and I soon realised I couldn't glory in the moment until we'd actually done the job we'd come to Wembley to do and win the first trophy in Stoke City's long and illustrious history.

I USED TO buy the Charlie Buchan weekly magazine when I was a lad. I would read about Stanley Matthews and picture myself playing like him – on the wing. I was lucky. I'd actually seen him play for the Football League against the League of Ireland at Dalymount Park in Dublin. I lived only 400 yards away from the ground, so I was able to see Stan play that day. He was the ultimate hero for every boy at that time and he was the man for me. That of course meant that Stoke City were a big club, although I never really supported a particular team as a kid. I was more into big players like Matthews and Finney.

There were ten kids in my family, eight boys and two girls. I was the second youngest and from a very early age I grew up with my older brothers playing football at League of Ireland level. All my brothers had played for a very famous junior club called Home Farm. It has produced countless players to have gone on to have careers in football and played for the Republic, including the likes of Graham Kavanagh. I followed in their footsteps and got into the B team at the age of 11, where I was two years younger than the lads I was playing against. But I was small and scrawny and it wasn't until I grew a bit up to the age of 17 that people sat up and took notice of me.

When I was 18 I had to make a decision as to whether I continued my seven-year apprenticeship in the printing industry, which was the family trade, or tried to make it in football. Obviously my mind was really on football and an offer came in from an Irish League club, Glentoran, in Northern Ireland. They offered me a contract and I thought I'd have a better chance of being spotted by an English club if I went there. There was also another issue for me. The League of Ireland played their games on Sundays, but the Irish League played on Saturdays and I reckoned that my weekend would be wrecked if I had to wait to play on Sunday. My Saturday night out would be ruined!

So now I was a professional and I made something of an impression at Glentoran. As luck would have it, the manager of Ards was George Eastham, who was the father of Stoke's George Eastham. George was Tony Waddington's eyes and ears in Ireland and he told him about me and how I was beginning to attract attention from Football League scouts. Most had said that I was too skinny and not tall enough, but Waddo liked skill in a player and George knew that. But at that stage Waddo didn't do anything.

The first big offer I had came when I had the chance to go to Fulham. Their manager Vic Buckingham turned up after a cup tie we'd drawn against Derry City. Vic was Arthur Daley reincarnated. He really was. He was a charming and persuasive cockney and he'd already agreed terms with Glentoran and was telling me about how wonderful things were going to be when I signed for Fulham. But I thought he was overpowering. I should have been delighted, but I wasn't, because I didn't want to go to London. London didn't really appeal to me, even though Fulham were a First Division club. I just felt I'd be lost. Anyway the local paper at home was full of headlines about the move and the £10,000 fee that Fulham were to pay, but because I was unsure, I hadn't actually said I'd go. George Eastham read the headlines and got straight on the blower to Tony Waddington and told him to come over sharpish.

So Waddo turned up to watch the cup replay against Derry, but as it happened there was a huge snowfall that day and the game was postponed. I'd travelled all the way up from home in Dublin and I was waiting for a train to go back again when who should turn up but George Eastham. I said, "Hello. Mr Eastham."

"Hello, Terry," he said. "I'd like you to meet the manager of Stoke City, Tony Waddington. He's come to see the game tonight, but now it's postponed he's going to fly home from Dublin. Do you mind if he travels back with you." That was a classic tap up, you know!

And on the train Waddo was telling me how I couldn't go to Fulham because Stoke was a much more homely club and all this chat. He was a silver-tongued devil, but I liked him. So I invited him to meet my father and they had a whiskey together. And when Waddo had gone my father was telling me how he was such a nice man and how he'd look after me. He was as gullible as me!

So it all got arranged. Fulham weren't very happy as they'd been gazumped, but Waddo had got his man. My personal terms were £30 a week and £15 for first team appearances. I'd been on £7 a week at the printers and another £10 for playing for Glentoran, so I'd more than doubled my money. What was funny was that Waddo always told people he'd had his eye on me for years – when in fact he'd never even seen me play!

I ARRIVED IN Stoke in March 1967. John Mahoney signed the day before me and then two weeks later Waddo signed Gordon Banks. The other two became regular first teamers straight away, but I didn't feature until October. It was partly because I was so skinny and Tony wanted to build me up. Now he was a great publicist and he told the papers that I was being put on a diet of Guinness and steak. Even today I think I'm the only Irishman that doesn't drink Guinness! He would also say that I was the seventh son of a seventh son. Well, I am the seventh son, but my Dad wasn't! But he would use every opportunity to build me, the team and the club up.

I remember another occasion just after I joined when I attended a supporters evening along with Waddo and I remember him standing up introducing me as the new signing and I was smiling at all the supporters in the room and then he finished up by saying, "And now Terry will give us a song"! Now as anyone will tell you, I am not a singer, but I stood up and gave a rendition of Danny Boy. Then I became the 'singing Irishman' in the newspapers! All the journalists loved Waddo because he would give them stories and make their jobs easy, so they made his life easy and the club got a great press. He would always be in the *News of the World* or the *Mirror* making bids for Wyn Davies or Ron Davies or George Best. And because of that he gave the people of Stoke dreams. People believed in him and he had the vision to give them what they wanted.

OF COURSE WHAT Stoke fans craved more than anything was to win something. Waddo had assembled a team that was capable of doing so. We had some fantastic players. The back four were all local lads. Even in those days that was a bit unique as players had been moving around for a long time by then. Denis Smith, Mike Pejic and Jackie Marsh had all just established themselves at the time. They were hard, hard men and when you add Alan 'Bluto' Bloor into that back four you got some X-rated tackles, you really did.

George Eastham was a classy player, who had played at the very top level. He had a cultured left foot, although he was coming towards the end of his career. Alongside George, we had real driving midfielders like John Mahoney and Micky Bernard, who were real box to box players; real midfield dynamos.

It was a great blend. This was what Waddo had spent all his years in charge building up to. That team picked itself for about four years from 1970 to 1973. It was all about continuity. People can still reel off the names now. There were really only a dozen or so players in contention and then the ones around the fringes like Sean Haslegrave, Danny Bowers and Eric Skeels. It wasn't until players like Eastham and Dobing retired that the likes of Huddy and Geoff Salmons came in.

I made the breakthrough into the first team in October 1967 when I was lucky enough to score on my debut against Leicester, the winning goal in a 3-2 win, but I only played ten games that season. I was getting a bit more confident being around these great players. I was in awe of them really. I wouldn't dare speak to them in case they didn't say hello back. You wouldn't think it now, would you?

But in the summer of 1968 Waddo put me into the mix in the first team proper. He always said he had a long-term plan with me, but I think he was just covering his tracks in case I didn't work out. Waddo wasn't big on tactics. Not a huge tactician at all. About the only thing he would do is ask someone like John Mahoney or Micky Bernard or Eric Skeels to man-mark the opponents' midfield dangerman. Other than that he would just say, "Go out there and enjoy yourselves. We've got the players to damage anyone. We are as good as any other team." And he was right. We would always give teams like Liverpool and Leeds a great game, although sometimes those more physical sides could overpower us towards the end of games. Then factors like the crowd and intimidation of officials would come to bear as well.

Some of the stuff we played was wonderful. It really was; off the cuff, creative, dynamic and attacking. The understanding between Ritchie and Greenhoff up front was remarkable. They played so well together and I was able to bring some dribbling and crossing into that mix. I was unpredictable in that even I didn't know what I was going to do next. That was an asset because it meant people couldn't man-mark me out of the game as we interchanged position a lot and weren't rigid in our attacking shape.

We all worked hard on our game. I was naturally right-footed, but after a while my left foot was nearly as good. I actually preferred to play out on the left because I thought it gave me a great advantage in that it gave me the option of either cutting inside on my right foot or going outside on my left. If you've only got one foot you'll be channelled down your weaker side constantly by any decent defender. But I could go either way. In fact if you look at the League Cup final in 1972, the second goal actually came from me getting to the byline on the left wing and crossing to the back post.

But I'm getting ahead of myself. Cup runs don't start at Wembley. They normally start in some lower division ground and that was true for us. We drew Southport away in round two. There was actually a big crowd there for them of over 10,000 and Southport gave us a decent game. We won 2-1, but only after a battle. Jimmy Greenhoff scored the winner from Ritchie's cross. I didn't play, but I was at the game and remember it being tough.

In the third round we pulled Second Division Oxford out of the hat. We drew 1-1 at the old Manor Ground. We were lucky there. It was a very sloping pitch and it was another battle; a real scrap. I don't think anyone was too enamoured with the result, but we hadn't lost. When you play lower league opposition they are always up for the fight and it's difficult to play football against them. They try to bring you down to their level and both games against Oxford were like that. But we won 2-0 at home, although that wasn't really settled until Sean Haslegrave netted a good volley right at the death.

But then we drew one of the truly big teams in the fourth round; Manchester United at Old Trafford. We felt hard done by in that game because John Ritchie scored a perfectly good goal which was disallowed. We were by far the better team that night, but we only came away with a 1-1 draw because Alan Gowling netted a header with about five minutes to go..

I remember George Eastham, Gordon Banks and Bobby Charlton used to socialise a lot because they'd all been in the triumphant World Cup squad in 1966. And George and Gordon would always come back and tell us how much Bobby said United hated playing against Stoke. We used to love playing them. That particular tie ran to three games, and extra time in both the replays before it was decided, but we were pretty much the better team throughout. Then, don't forget, we drew in them in our run to the FA Cup semi-final as well. Again we drew at their place, but won at home in extra time and I scored the winning goal. There were over 49,000 people inside the Vic that night. It was electrifying.

In the League Cup we beat them in the second replay at the Vic. We won thanks to a very late John Ritchie goal from George Eastham's cross. It was a dream for Stoke fans. To knock United out was massive and the elation after that set us thinking. Now we were saying, "Well, you never know." And when Bristol Rovers came out of the hat in the quarter-final we really began to believe.

There was a colossal spirit in the side and there were no shirkers. Everyone had to do their job and if you didn't you felt guilty. Normally two or three of us would be strapped up so that you could be part of it - Smithy seemed to be permanently bandaged up! I remember him breaking two fingers in scoring his goal at Bristol Rovers in the quaerter-final. You never wanted to miss a game because it was such a joy to be playing.

WE PLAYED VERY, very well at Eastville. We quickly went 4-0 up and were strolling about on a pudding of a pitch. I remember scoring the fourth goal after Greenhoff, Smith and a rare Micky Bernard strike had put us comfortably ahead. Rovers got two late goals, but we were never in trouble. They had been really primed for that game, but sometimes we just really clicked and that night it was a joy. They were chasing shadows to be honest and there was only going to be one winner. I remember we all went out to a night club after that win. It wasn't often we did that away from home, but to get to a semi-final was terrific and we celebrated on that occasion!

So that set us up for a two-legged semi-final with West Ham. They had great players like Geoff Hurst, Trevor Brooking, Harry Redknapp, Billy Bonds and, of course, Bobby Moore. We wanted to earn a two-goal lead from our home leg to take down to Upton Park. That was the plan. We felt if we drew at home in the first leg it would be a killer to our hopes of getting to Wembley. So when we scored early on we thought we were home and hosed, but then devastated wasn't the word when they came back to win. Clyde Best scored an equaliser and then won a penalty which Hursty belted home past Gordon Banks to win the game. A 2-1 defeat at home seemed to put us right out of it. We really were devastated. All our dreams seemed in tatters. I felt we'd blown it, that it had gone. But how wrong I was.

We travelled down to stay the night before the return leg at a hotel in Grays in Essex and trained on the Tuesday afternoon. Afterwards something slightly strange happened. We felt refreshed and suddenly the belief surged back into us. People were walking around the hotel saying that we fancied ourselves to win. Somehow or other we were all believing that we were going to win. The closer the game got, the more positive we became. I don't know where it came from because we'd been outplayed in the first leg, but I think we all realised it was because we hadn't performed in that game, rather than West Ham being so brilliant. Now we thought we couldn't be so bad again.

That inner belief allowed us to take the game to them at Upton Park. They felt they were home and dry and maybe relaxed a bit too much. We played really well and then a cross from the right found itself to the back post where John Ritchie turned and lashed it back across Bobby Ferguson in the West Ham goal. So it was now 2-2 on aggregate. Away goals did not count double in those days, so we knew that the chances were the next goal would win the game.

It was end to end stuff and both sides had some good chances, but then, two minutes before the end, came the moment that will live in Stoke City history forever when Gordon Banks proved, if there was any doubt, that he was the greatest goalkeeper in the world. Mind you, Gordon had to pull something out of the bag because it was he who pulled Harry Redknapp down after a mix-up between himself and Mike Pejic to give away a last gasp penalty. We were giving Banksy some fearful stick for a few seconds before we left him to prepare, but I think all that was stored up inside him when Geoff Hurst put the ball down on the spot to take the penalty. Half the players on the pitch couldn't bear to look. Some of us had already mentally given up. Disconsolate wasn't the word. I couldn't see any way back if it went in as there wasn't much time left. The tension was unbelievable. And it was the two World Cup heroes, Hurst versus Banks. Hursty took this long run up for his penalties and he always hit them hard, so off he sets, and I remember standing at the edge of the box as he ran up, and nobody would have thought that Banksy would have saved it, especially against Geoff. Then Geoff belted it and I thought, 'That's it.' And then disbelief – because Hurst didn't miss penalties, he just didn't miss them. And somehow Banksy had twisted to his left, when he'd begun to go the wrong way, and flicked the ball with his hand over the bar. It all happened in a flash and we ran to Banksy and patted him on the back a bit cock-a-hoop really, but then realised we had to face a corner! It was a truly phenomenal save and one of the most crucial in the club's history. His reactions were incredible. Somehow he'd saved us and that built the belief even more.

THE FIRST REPLAY was a poor affair at Hillsborough; a 0-0 draw after extra time. We were having to drag our bodies through it all and it was January and the pitches were heavy and took their toll. League games were continuing and the FA Cup had started up as well, so it was very tough and the games were coming thick and fast then and it's perhaps no surprise that one of these games was a stinker. But didn't we make up for it in the fourth match at Old Trafford?!

It was a typical Manchester day, raining all day before the game and puddles all over the pitch. Once again there was penalty controversy when Micky Bernard's kick was saved by the keeper – who happened to be Bobby Moore because Ferguson had had to go off with concussion because yours truly had kicked him in the head accidentally chasing a through ball! Thankfully Micky hit home the rebound to put us 1-0 ahead. It was one of the most unbelievable decisions of all time for West Ham to put the best defender in the world in goal. I still to this day cannot fathom that one out. It gave us a lift to see Bobby pulling on the green jersey, it really did. He was still captain of England, the leader, and they put him in goal.

Then West Ham came back after Ferguson returned between the sticks and scored twice to lead 2-1. It was an incredible game of ebb and flow, played in this horrendous sticky mud and right on half-time Peter Dobing levelled the score once again.

The second half was a phenomenal tussle and one which I think we won through sheer bloody-mindedness. There were times when we were splashing through puddles and the ball was sticking, but I was fortunate in that it fell to me to score the goal that took the club to Wembley for the first time in its history. I just hit this shot and it fair flew in from the edge of the box. It was actually only just after half-time, so we didn't know it was going to be the winner as there was still so long to play and there had been so many twists and turns already that you didn't want to assume anything any more.

The elation at the final whistle was incredible. The joy on Gordon Banks' face was amazing to see. You know, he'd won nothing at club level despite appearing in an FA Cup final and a League Cup final with Leicester, and now he'd got to another final. To say he was pretty pleased would be an understatement. Waddo had made a promise to Banksy when he signed for the club that he would win things at Stoke and now he had the chance.

After the game, Ron Greenwood, the West Ham manager, accused me of deliberately injuring the goalkeeper Ferguson. But I wasn't physically capable of doing that and I certainly wasn't going to do it on purpose. I never wore shinpads and there was some heavy bruising on my shin which showed where his head had come into contact with me at speed. So I was almost as hurt as he was, but I had no intention to do him harm. That disappointed me.

THERE'S A LOT of stuff which surrounds playing in a Wembley final. The build up to the game was unbelievable. Waddo was great to us. Our allocation of tickets for the game was 200 each! That was colossal. We paid for them, they weren't given free, but nowadays they get a very small allocation. I used up over 100 of those in Ireland bringing family and friends over, some of whom had never left Ireland before and quite a few of those were more into hurling than football. Waddo had obviously thought about this and didn't want any lingering problems of anyone phoning up players trying to scrounge tickets, which was very sensible as when you've got to a Wembley final it's amazing how many long lost cousins and uncles come out of the woodwork!

Then, of course, there was the Jackie Trent and Tony Hatch song We'll Be With You, which the team recorded and got to No. 35 in the charts. I was actually away with Ireland on international duty and missed the recording, so was more than happy to make up for it by giving my infamous rendition of the song in the bath after the final for the TV cameras! I do remember at the rehearsals Tony Hatch had to eliminate one or two of the boys from the line-up because they were tone deaf and he couldn't work out why it sounded so bad until he weeded out the culprits.

There were newspaper articles and radio interviews to do. We went along with it all because we were suddenly in the limelight and that hadn't happened before. I remember one morning going on to Noel Edmonds' show on BBC Radio 1 with a couple of the other lads and having a good laugh because Noel revealed he was a Chelsea supporter. There was a huge amount of interest for the whole month before it.

I was doing pieces in the *Mirror* with a lad called Vince Wilson. One day he said that he wanted something that was a bit controversial and he asked me if I'd ever had any abuse when I played in London, and so I said that at West Ham I'd been called a ginger-haired, carrot-topped Irishman, and been told to, "Go back to the bog." It was all part and parcel of the banter as far as I was concerned. Well Vince wanted to turn this into a Chelsea story and asked me if there was anyone I didn't like in the Chelsea team. As it happened I didn't really like Peter Osgood, so Vince said, "We'll call him Mr X." So in the paper there was this column about how I wanted to win the cup against Chelsea so that I could turn round to this Mr X and tell him how it was to shut him up for all this abuse he'd given me over the years. Totally made up.

So the article appears and I promise you that it's the god's honest truth that as we were going down the tunnel before the game at Wembley, Paddy Mulligan and John Dempsey, with whom I played for Ireland and knew well, said, "TC, who's this Mr X?" They both wanted to know if it was them! So I said, "No. Of course it's not you." And John Hollins was behind them and he wanted to know too. They'd obviously all got wound up by it!

Thankfully they never worked out either who I didn't like, or how the article came about. In the years before he died I met Ossie at several dinners and I couldn't have found him a more approachable and charming guy, but back then he was nauseating.

WE STAYED DOWN at the Selsdon Park Hotel in Surrey in the days leading up to the game and just played five-a-side all week. No one ever mentioned the final. Banksy wanted to play at centre-forward all the time and it was very competitive, but at the same time very relaxed. We didn't worry about Chelsea in particular and Waddo didn't give us a team plan. Why should he? We'd got where we were by playing the way we always did, so why change now?

Jackie Trent and Tony Hatch only lived a mile from the hotel in Surrey, and we were invited to go round for a drink one night, so a group of us went to see them with the manager in tow. It turned out they were throwing a bit of a party with celebrities there and a few nice looking girls and plenty of booze. It was the Wednesday night and the temptation was strong, very strong. Maybe Waddo was testing us and our professionalism, but we just stayed for an hour and nobody got up to anything untoward. But who would have thought a manager would place that temptation in front of his players three days before the biggest game in the club's history?

As we got closer to the final the keenness amongst us in training increased a few notches. I remember on the Friday morning the five-a-side looked as if it could have got out of hand. That was healthy as long as it didn't spill over and Waddo called the session off when it all got a bit on edge. I do remember one occasion before a big game that it did get out of hand. It was in the lead-up to the FA Cup semi-final that same season. We were staying at a hotel near Hillsborough before we met Arsenal and in a five-a-side match on the Friday before the game, the tension spilt over and John Mahoney and Gordon Banks had a bit of a set-to. Fists flew and the pair had to be separated, but it showed just how much it meant to everyone involved. It's a very passionate time in the build up to major matches like that and things can happen.

Finally the day of the game arrived. All the people at the hotel lined the drive to see us off, staff and residents. That was nice. I can't remember much of the journey across London to Wembley as I was focussing on the game ahead, but I remember it went quickly.

Wembley was packed with Stoke fans. It was a wonderful sight. I remember that as we walked up that long tunnel at the old Wembley we could hear the buzz of the crowd growing louder and louder like an enormous swarm of bees. I never really got nervous before games. I could take it all in my stride. Marshy always got very wound up and Pej was the same, but I was lucky to be of that disposition. Seeing all the fans brought a lump to my throat. It looked magnificent. That number of people had never watched a Stoke team play before. I'd only been to see one game at Wembley myself, the 1967 FA Cup Final between Spurs and Chelsea, so it was all new.

My goal came early on. It was strange because it was a nothing build-up. A long throw came in and somehow the ball found its way to me about eight yards out. It came looping across and I just put my head on it and the next thing I knew there was all this noise and I saw the ball in the back of the net. I'd scored. It wasn't contrived by a great flowing move, or a piece of skill, it just sort of happened in a very scrappy way. But I suppose in cup finals it doesn't matter who scores or how they go in. All that matters is what's on that scoreboard.

After the goal I was in a daze and every time I was given the ball I just gave it away. I was useless for five or even ten minutes after that. My mind kept being drawn to that scoreboard, 'Conroy 4'. It was an eerie experience, it really was and I felt it was a culmination of all those years of hard work, all those years of striving and working and wanting to be the best I could. I had replicated my dreams, the kinds of dreams that millions of kids have. I had done it.

Thank god for Jackie Marsh shaking me out of it. He got me going again otherwise the team would have been one short. I wasn't in touch with the game for those minutes.

Mind you, to make the perfect story you have to score the winner, don't you? But I got it wrong. I scored the first goal. I made up for that, though, because I helped make the second.

CHELSEA EQUALISED JUST on half-time when Osgood hooked the ball in from a prone position lying on the ground when we should have cleared the ball and we trudged into the dressing rooms when we should have been skipping in with a 1-0 lead. I still maintain that Chelsea were the better side on the day and they created more chances, but it was a real end to end game all through the second half. It was up and down for 90 minutes, two attacking teams. There was no lull, no period of stalemate. I didn't feel we played as well and as fluently as we could. But defensively we were superb. We weren't so good going forward and in midfield they overpowered us a bit, but the game is about taking chances – and we took two.

The winning goal came when Peter Dobing knocked a ball 40 yards across to me. I just had it in my mind to attack the blue jersey in front of me and I got by David Webb on the left wing and crossed to the back post where I knew where John would be, he was always at the far post. Ritchie nodded it down to Greeenhoff, who was about 12 yards out. Jimmy volleyed it towards goal, but Peter Bonetti pulled off a wonderful save, diving to his right. But he couldn't hold on to the ball and it bounced out to where two Stoke players, Eastham and Dobing were waiting to stick it in the net. George won that particular race to prod the ball home. 2-1 Stoke.

There wasn't long to go then and we knew Chelsea would press us back, but actually the only real chance they had was one we created for them. I remember being right in line with Micky Bernard when he hit this pass back to Gordon Banks. Now in those days keepers could pick the ball up from backpasses, not like today, so Micky thought he was playing a safe pass, but it was short. Just outside the area the Chelsea forward Colin Garland latched on to the ball and was bearing down on goal, but then out of nowhere came Gordon Banks to put in the most ferocious challenge and send the ball to safety. That was a colossal save. It really was. I really sensed then that with the form Banksy was in Chelsea weren't going to score.

I remember another simple save he made from a header from a corner when less experienced keepers would have been shouting and bawling and wanting to try to punch crosses even if they couldn't reach them. The corner came across and he just caught the ball as if he was having a cup of tea. So calm and collected. Fantastic.

MY OVER-RIDING emotion at the end of the game wasn't so much that we'd won, more that I was so glad I didn't have to run any more. That Wembley pitch sapped the strength right out of your legs and it had been a very quick game and we'd all galloped a few miles. I just sat down. That was my first reaction. Just to sit down because I was drained, both physically and mentally.

Eventually the emotion kicked in that we had won and within a couple of minutes I was looking around and drinking it all in. And then we went up those steps. It's very hard to describe my feelings, because it was literally a dream come true. How many times can you say that's happened in your life?

We didn't get medals, we got tankards for some reason. And then Peter Dobing picked the cup up as captain and we toured it round the ground. That part of the day went very quickly and is something of a daze to be honest and I remember more about the dressing room afterwards. Of course singing We'll Be With You in the bath lives with me to this day because it was caught on film. That bit I haven't watched at all I can tell you, but my girls often take the mickey about it as my voice is so high-pitched and I had the mutton chop sideboards.

Then it was back to the Russell Hotel and the party began.

THERE'S NOT MANY times I dwell on the day of the final. It's a private thing and I've actually only watched the video four or five times, and then because I've been at screenings with fans. But I do appreciate what winning something meant to the supporters. It's always more special to the fans than it is for a player as we're not allowed to dwell on these things, so sometimes it feels like somebody else achieved that.

We had no idea what to expect when we came into Stoke. We got off the train at Barlaston and on to a really old charabanc. I remember going through Meir and Smithy and Bluto were very emotional at that point. Marshy felt the same when we got to Longton. Of course it was even more special for those local lads. It meant something extra special to win something for their club. I know how much it meant to me, so I can't imagine how good it must have felt for them. The mass of people who turned out to greet us was incredible. They seemed to be hundreds deep everywhere we went on the route down to the King's Hall. I only wish that ultimately we could have given those wonderful fans more of those occasions during our halcyon days.

DENIS SMITH: BORN 19 NOVEMBER 1947, STOKE-ON-TRENT 488 GAMES, 42 GOALS

Denis Smith

Ajax 0 Stoke City 0

UEFA Cup first round second leg

Wednesday 2 October 1974

I'M A STOKE LAD and I was always a Stoke City supporter through and through. It was in my blood. I'd been watching the team play since way before Matthews came back and there's not many people that can say that these days! I loved going down to the Victoria Ground and watching my heroes, like Eddie Stuart, Don Ratcliffe and Dennis Viollet.

I began my career representing Stoke-on-Trent schoolboys in the English Schools Shield alongside a few other players who made it in the game like Jackie Mash and Bill Bentley. We won the competition two years running in 1962 and 1963. I suppose that was as good a competition as the FA Youth Cup in those days, in which I also played for Stoke City as an amateur. We reached the final of the Youth Cup in 1961, losing to Everton, so we were an extremely successful young side.

While I was still an amateur, I worked as a plumber's mate for the Stoke chairman Percy Axon. That meant I got all the time off I needed to train and travel to matches. Because of the success we'd had, I actually got offered to be taken on as an apprentice by both Spurs and Portsmouth. Pompey had the best youth set-up in the country at the time, but I only had eyes for Stoke.

By the time I got to 18 I was considered good enough to be offered a contract, although I must admit Waddo wasn't overkeen when I went in to see him to demand that I be taken on full time. He said that he couldn't afford me, but I was only on £10 per game, while I was on £20 a week at work. So I asked, "Well, what can you pay me?"

"£12 a week."

"I'll take it."

I still got my appearance money, but I was down £8 a week for a while, so that gave me some incentive to make it into the first team. Fairly soon afterwards I was knocking on his door asking to be in the side.

Waddo actually took some convincing by the older players that I should be put in. I think he thought that because of where I came from – Meir being something of a rough area – that reflected on the kind of person I was; in other words that I was some kind of ragamuffin or scallion. I think it was only because they were fed up with playing against me in training that the senior players felt I should be given a chance, so eventually Waddo put me in against Arsenal in September 1968. After that I always felt I was the first name on the team sheet because I always gave total commitment.

Of course, having played for 14 years at Stoke, I took part in any number of great matches. There was the run to the victory in the League Cup, and, of course, it meant everything to me to win at Wembley. Then getting to the FA Cup semi-finals in both 1971 and 1972, that both ended in such disappointing defeat to Arsenal, saw us play some fantastic matches, particularly against Manchester United. Scoring the winning goal in the incredible 3-2 comeback win over Leeds in 1974, which ended their record 29-match unbeaten run from the start of the season, was a special moment for me. Then there was also the promotion season of 1978/79 and a successful battle against relegation in 1981/82, my last season at the club, when we won the final game against West Brom to save ourselves and send Leeds down.

But the reason I've chosen the UEFA Cup tie against Ajax is that I always wanted to test myself against the best. That was my raison d'être for playing top flight football. Pure and simple. This team had invented 'total football' and dominated Europe. They were the best.

We'd finished fifth in the First Division in 1973/74 thanks to a fine end of season run in when we won seven out of the last 11 games. Of course we had a wonderfully talented footballing team. The fulcrum was Alan Hudson, who on his day was as good as anyone in the country. Huddy passed and ran to receive return balls all day long and he prompted our strike force of John Ritchie and Jimmy Greenhoff into action. The pitch at the Victoria Ground was just a bog between the end of September and mid-April, so when banners started appearing around the stadium saying, 'Alan Hudson walks on water' they weren't joking! Huddy's arrival at the club in February 1974 had coincided with us hitting the kind of form that, had we signed him earlier in the season, would have seen us in with a shout of the League Championship. We were wallowing in 17th place when he joined, but by the end of the season we'd climbed up to to fifth.

We were scoring goals for fun as now Geoff Hurst had been added to the strike force, but when John Ritchie returned to the team late in the season, he scored a number of important goals, including a great hat-trick against Southampton in a 4-1 win at the Brit. I remember that game because it had been surrounded by a war of words in the press between Ritchie and Peter Osgood, who was never our favourite player, ever since his days at Chelsea.

Osgood had said something about how Ritchie couldn't score goals with his head, so for the third of his hat-trick he rounded the keeper, stopped the ball on the line, knelt down and headed it in! When the draw for the UEFA Cup paired us with Dutch giants Ajax, I relished the prospect of playing them. I really did fancy us as I knew our style of play would cause them problems. Yes, I knew they had won the European Cup for three successive seasons from 1971-1973, and provided the vast majority of the Dutch side which had reached the 1974 World Cup final – and should have won it. But Johann Cruyff and Johann Neeskens had been sold to Barcelona in the summer, so they weren't quite the force they had been.

There was a huge social scene around the club back then, as everyone I think knows. Most of the lads loved a drink or two, as did the manager, and it really did help bond a lot of the team together, but I wasn't really interested in all that. I didn't drink and I actually preferred to spend my spare time doing things like attending meetings of the Round Table where I talked to businessmen and learnt about that side of life. I've found it's helped me in my career as a manager with all the other aspects of the job outside pure footballing matters that are so important. It also gave me plenty of fresh ideas when it came to analysing the performance of players. Just little things, like when I was at West Brom I insisted that I be bought a laptop on which I kept the records of all my own players and was also able to analyse those I was interested in putting bids in for to sign. That was as late as 1997, so you can see how backward a big club like West Brom had been. Really it was all brought in because of the innovation of Arsène Wenger and I thought it was vital to be a part of that to keep up. Now, of course, Pro-zone and video analysis of players is standard.

FOR ME, HAVING been a manager for 25 years now, I want players who give me total commitment, because that means they fulfil their potential. Attitude is so important. That's what really makes the difference between what division players can play in. Talent is just one aspect of being a footballer. If you've got all the talent in the world and don't work at your game you won't make it as far as you should do. It's about desire and passion and that's something that's relatively rare these days. It's certainly what sets many so-called talented lower division players apart.

I like to think that I gave my all in every game I played. Sometimes I played better than others, of course, but it wasn't due to a lack of application.

Ajax may not have been able to field Cruyff or Neeskens in their line-up, but they certainly had a fair side. Ruud Krol and Arie Haan were wonderful midfielders and they also had the Muhren brothers as well. Arnold Muhren became more well known over here with his skills and superb left foot during spells at Ipswich Town and Manchester United. Up front Johnny Rep was the golden boy of Dutch football. His goal had won the third of those European Cup finals against Juventus in 1973. In goal they had international keeper Piet Schrijvers, so it was a top quality side.

Waddo was a magnificent publicist. In the build-up to the game he revealed publicly that he'd had the opportunity to sign Johann Cruyff when he was aged just 19. The story ran that a pilot friend of his had seen Cruyff play whilst on a rest day having flown to

Holland. Waddo had put a bid in, but then had realised that the work permit regulations in existence at the time meant Cruyff could not join a British club. What a signing that would have been, although that could well have been another one of Waddo's famous tall tales! Ajax's manager, Hans Kraay, was relatively young. He was in his first season in the job and followed several high profile figures who had been in charge of the club during its rise to European prominence. Rinus Michels, who went on to manage Holland in the 1974 World Cup, had won the first two European Cups. Then Stefan Kovacs had overseen what was considered a failure of a campaign because they'd only ended up in the UEFA Cup. So Kraay was relatively new to the job. He was actually only 37-years-old and a former Dutch international himself. Also his coaching CV included a spell in charge of the Dutch international hockey team. New though he may be, Kraay had made a very positive impact on the club as they had won every single game they had competed in so far in that season. That was quite a record to take on for us.

THE BUILD UP to the game was a typical cat and mouse affair with both managers playing their cards close to their chests. Both chose not to announce their teams in advance. Kraay did admit he thought it was a tricky draw for his team and called for seeding to be introduced to the competition, which now does exist, to ensure that strong teams wouldn't meet until the later rounds.

Of their usual line-up Jan Mulder, a £200,000 signing from Belgian club Anderlecht, missed the first leg due to a suspect knee. They were also without Wim Suurbier, the Dutch international full-back, who was injured.

On our side, Huddy played with a broken hand, damaged when he crashed his car a couple of weeks earlier. He'd been out on a drinking session with the manager, who also liked to have a pint or two, and had gone off the road on the way home. Typical Huddy really.

After the devastation of our last foray into Europe, following our victory in the 1972 League Cup final, when we'd been hammered 4-0 in Kaiserslautern after winning the home leg 3-1, we really wanted a two-goal lead to take to Amsterdam if possible, but knew it would be very tough. We actually fielded the same back six in both legs against Ajax as had played in Kaiserslautern – Farmer, Marsh, Pejic, myself, Bloor and Mahoney as the defensive midfielder – so we had plenty to make up for.

The problem was we couldn't get the ball off Ajax. They were in charge for the vast majority of the first leg and gave us a bit of a lesson in controlling an away game in Europe. They were clinical, played keep ball and they got to the crowd. In attack they played neat patterns and kept the ball away from us, looking to simply steal a single away goal, while in defence, they used the most annoying spoiling tactic there is; the offside trap. Our crowd rarely had seen a team play like that and they didn't particularly like it. Neither did we, but we were finding it difficult to do anything about it.

Ajax moved forward with such pace and skill and eventually, almost inevitably, I suppose, a quick one-two between Rep and Krol saw some space open up and Krol hit this fantastic shot, which zipped into the net past John Farmer.

Krol was Huddy's man and Alan knows that he should have closed him down, but he wasn't quite on his game that night because of his car crash.

Huddy now claims that we'd have beaten Ajax if he hadn't had that smash, but they were so good that night, so much in control, that I'm not sure that even a fully fit and firing Hudson would have made that much difference.

He was much quieter than usual going forward, although we didn't create much at all as a team in the first hour to be honest. Dusvaba hardly left Greenhoff's side and kept Jimmy as quiet as anyone I ever saw.

Finally, with 15 minutes to go, we managed to get a foothold in the game. From a free kick Mike Pejic hit a left foot shot, but it was touched against the post by Schrijvers. I'd been in the penalty area in case the ball was crossed in and had followed in after the ball, so I lunged in to prod it over line, leaving my marker, Dusvaba, sprawled on the ground in the process.

We did put them under some pressure after that with some early crosses into the box and plenty more set pieces, and they were looking to hang on to the draw. I should have had a hat-trick with the crosses we put in to be honest. Ajax didn't like that approach to the game and we unsettled them a bit, but essentially they were in control that night, although we felt we now knew enough about them to give them a good game over in Holland.

I was fairly battered and bruised after that match and had to have three stitches in a cut just below my eye which I'd done lunging in to score the goal, but I had loved the competitive nature of the game and the cut and thrust of European competition. It was football at the highest level.

In between the two legs of the tie, we hit a poor patch of form. As luck would have it, the fixture list gave us away matches against the top two teams in the league, Liverpool and Ipswich, within three days. Despite being fourth ourselves, we lost both games, 3-0 at Anfield and 3-1 at Portman Road. Worse still, at Ipswich, John Ritchie broke his leg following a dreadful tackle by Kevin Beattie and then Alan Dodd got himself sent off.

John's career was ended by that leg break and having broken my own countless times during my own career, I felt for him. He may have been in the veteran stages of his career, but he still had a great eye for goal and had a wonderful relationship with Jimmy Greenhoff. We missed him.

We played much better on the following Saturday at home to Derby and should have won that game, but we only scored one goal – thanks to Ritchie's replacement Geoff Hurst – despite all our attacking, and Derby nicked a late equaliser.

Waddo had sent Gordon Banks and George Eastham to watch Ajax in their intervening games, so we knew exactly what to expect. Ajax had switched the game to the Olympic Stadium from their own Stadion de Meer, I think because they could accommodate more fans there. We felt it gave us more of a chance because it was effectively a neutral venue.

There was one slight problem on the way over when Geoff Salmons got to the airport to find he'd left his passport at home. They let him out of England OK, but we had to get special dispensation to allow him into the country when we arrived in Holland! He had to get the passport couriered over the next day and present it to officials to ensure he could stay.

The other controversy was caused by the presence in our party of Brian Clough, recently sacked by Leeds after just 44 days in the job. He was there as an observer, at Waddo's invitation. I'd like to think that what he learnt on that trip stood him in good stead to do so well with Derby in European competition and then win the European Cup with Forest. That really was a remarkable achievement. There were rumours in the press that Waddo was going to find a way to bring him to the Vic, but Clough was always too much of his own man to even consider taking an assistant's role, so I think that was just paper talk.

Waddo was always low key before such big games. We stayed out of town in a new skyscraper hotel and relaxed by going bowling and to the cinema the night before the game.

The Dutch press were terribly arrogant towards us. For them the result was a foregone conclusion. Ajax would win easily and little Stoke would be sent packing. Well, that's not how it quite turned out.

The other motivating factor for us was that everywhere we went we heard a version of the Chelsea song Blue Is The Colour, which they'd had written for the 1972 League Cup Final, that we'd won, of course, but with the words altered to say Ajax. Was that an omen? Fortunately domestic suspensions do not count in Europe, so Doddy was able to take his place alongside me despite his sending off at Ipswich and so the only change to our team was Geoff Hurst replacing Terry Conroy. We also played in a new away kit, which had a diagonal double black stripe running from the shoulder down to the waist on a yellow background with sky blue shorts. Unlike the Dutch, who'd only brought around 50 fans to the Victoria Ground, we had over 1,500 Stokies travelling with us, selling out the ticket allocation. That was a fantastic showing and tells you all you need to know about Stoke supporters.

Having been caught a bit at Stoke by their offside trap, we were now prepared for the way Ajax played, although we didn't expect them to rely on it so heavily at home. Waddo had taken it as a compliment that Ajax had chosen to play that way against us at Stoke as they were obviously worried at our attacking strength, so we felt they might be a bit over confident and leave some gaps for us to exploit at home.

THE GAME GOT off to an explosive start when Pej and Van Santen were both booked after a squabble near the touchline. It was the usual Pej thing, he was always getting himself into trouble. He was very intense. Geoff Hurst got booked early on too, I think for protesting about having his shirt pulled. I was soon in the wars again, this time I needed two more stitches when I gashed my knee, but we soon settled down to play some good football.

They always say that you should aim to silence the home fans in away legs and that's exactly what we did. It was what Ajax had done to us. They had thought this game would be a walkover, but so far we were the better side. The closest we came was when Josh Mahoney surged past three defenders, but had his run ended right on the edge of the area, when he was about to shoot. Josh had a great shot in either foot and often scored from the edge of the box, but he was stopped by a great tackle.

After half-time, when they'd had a chance to regroup a bit, Ajax began to hit back. They were too good to be completely out of the game. Farmer made a flying save from a Haan volley and saved point blank from Mulder, cutting in off the wing. But we were still giving as good as we got as the game got stretched a bit. Haslegrave brought a fine save from Schrijvers with a 15-yard shot and then Jimmy Greenhoff swerved a 20-yarder just past the post.

It was a really good game and Huddy, Sammy and Josh were getting the upper hand in midfield. They began to create panic in the Dutch defence as it became obvious that one goal would steal the game, but the best chances came late on. First Schrijvers had to scramble back on to his line to tip over a Greenhoff chip. Then, after he had come on as a substitute, Terry Conroy got to the byline and curled a cross against the bar. We were so close, but nothing had quite dropped for us in their box.

Then, right at the death, came the moment that so nearly won us the game. As we pressed forward and Ajax looked to defend their away goal lead, the ball bobbled around their penalty area before falling to our other substitute, Jimmy Robertson. He was about six yards out and only had the keeper to beat. The ball fell really nicely to him on the half volley, but he slipped slightly as he struck it and didn't get a full contact. His point blank shot hit the flailing

Schrijvers on the left boot and ricocheted to safety. We were inches from taking the lead. Only that outstretched boot saved them from defeat.

Shortly after that, amidst some last minute scrambles in the penalty area, TC shot over from about eight yards with only the keeper to beat. It was agonising. We had so nearly got the goal that would have put us through and sent Ajax crashing to only their second ever European home defeat. Their fans were whistling for the referee to blow for full time for about the last ten minutes they were so worried. Hans Kraay admitted he hadn't enjoyed the game at all as he'd been very nervous that we would win.

AFTERWARDS I FELT that we had done so well that, although I was obviously disappointed that we had gone out of the competition, we had proved a massive point that we could compete at the highest level. It was a shame that all most Stoke fans ever saw of the game was some very short TV highlights, which didn't do us justice at all as they just showed three or four missed chances, rather than the domination of the game we'd had.

I prefer to remember what Brian Clough said to us after the game, "It deserved to be the final. It was that good."

Sometimes you don't know what you've done as a player, what you've achieved. You don't understand what it means to the fans; what they're feeling, whether it be good or bad, but that night we exceeded everyone's expectations and delighted ourselves and that fantastic band of travelling fans. The myth was that the Dutch were masters of 'total football' and we destroyed that.

PAUL MAGUIRE: BORN 21 AUGUST 1956, GLASGOW; 120 GAMES, 25 GOALS

Paul Maguire

Stoke City 3 Leeds United 0

League Division One

Saturday 6 September 1980

I WAS FIRST on to the plane. I walked up the steps on to the Gulf Air jet bound for the Arab Emirates to play a hastily arranged friendly, and when I reached the top I could either turn left into first class, or right into standard. Needless to say, being Stoke, we were in economy. But I ventured a glance into first class and there, with a magnum of champagne already on the go, was Alan Hudson. He said, "Come on lads. Come and have a drink. Let's face it. It's not the European Cup is it?!"

And I thought, "You'll do for me!"

Nottingham Forest had pulled out of a trip to Abu Dhabi to play the Saudi Arabian team and there was a large financial incentive for Stoke to fill the gap, even though we'd got a match against Arsenal at home three days later. Finances were always tight at Stoke. So we flew out on the Wednesday morning to play the game that afternoon and then had an eight-hour trip back! There had been rumours Alan was coming to the club and that was our introduction to him. He was a great guy and a great character. I have never laughed so much in all my life as I did with him! He changed the face of Stoke City.

To cap that week, we beat Arsenal 1-0 at home on the Saturday and I scored the winning penalty after Sammy McIlroy was tripped. That was the start of one of the most incredible recoveries to escape relegation that any side anywhere has pulled off and it climaxed with me scoring four goals to keep the club in the First Division.

I am sure that everyone would think that Wolves game, when I scored the four goals to keep Stoke from being relegated to the

Second Division on the final day of the 1983/84 season would be a banker for me to choose as my greatest game. Obviously it was an important match and I'm not saying that scoring four goals wasn't fantastic, but for me the best feeling I ever had after a game was actually my debut, when we hammered Leeds United 3-0. It was the day I felt I had arrived at Stoke in the First Division. I caused havoc to Leeds, scored a cracking free-kick, the fans were singing my name and I felt on top of the world afterwards. It was truly amazing.

I HAD BEEN at Shrewsbury for four years and we'd had probably the best team in the club's history. We won the Third Division ahead of Swansea and Watford, who went on to go up to the First Division, and we reached the quarter-finals of the FA Cup in 1978/79, where we only narrowly lost to Wolves. CHECK?? We had players like Ian Atkins, Sammy Chapman, Graham Turner, the player-manager, Jimmy Livesey and Steve Biggins, who played up front with me. They weren't big names, but they had a lot of quality as many went on to play in the top flight.

Prior to Graham Turner, Alan Durban had been the Shrewsbury manager. He'd actually started as player-manager after leaving Derby, where he'd been part of the Brian Clough team which had won the league title. He'd moved on to Stoke after the club had been relegated in 1977 and turned the team around by mixing the good kids who'd been developed by Tony Waddington, with some good players that he brought in himself. Brendan O'Callaghan arrived from Doncaster Rovers, where he'd been scoring goals as a classic centre-forward, midfielder Howard Kendall arrived as player-coach and Mike Doyle, a very experienced centre-half, signed from Manchester City.

Today's game is all about pace and fitness. That was important when I played, but in our day it was as much about skill. Unless you've got serious pace these days you won't make the Premiership. You only have to look at someone like Robbie Fowler, who scored hundreds of goals, but since he lost that extra yard of pace he hasn't been able to make any impression. At Leeds and Manchester City and now back at Liverpool, he's barely played let alone scored.

Back in 1980, Stoke had just sold Garth Crooks after he had helped win promotion in 1979. He'd had a good first season up in the First Division, where Stoke were now a small fish in a bigger pond. Without Garth, though, Stoke lacked some pace, and I was quick. Not as lightning fast as Garth, but over a short sprint I could beat a man and make enough space to get a cross in for Big Bren to attack the ball. So Durban knew me and what I could do and when I became dissatisfied at Shrewsbury he came in for me. He knew that he had a side with great ability, but quite a young side that lacked certain attributes. There were young players who had come up through the youth team like Paul Bracewell, Adrian Heath and Lee Chapman in the side, who were just beginning to make an impression in the top flight. They obviously all went on to great things, sadly for Stoke elsewhere, but the talent they had was developed in those years at Stoke.

With the money that Durban had got for Crooks (£650,000), he had already signed left-back Peter Hampton and Iain Munro as left-sided midfielder and so he had a totally new left-hand side of the team when I arrived. He'd actually spent over £1m in his two years in charge.

Durban first contacted me about the possibility of coming to Stoke at the Midland Player of the Year awards in March 1980 and we talked about the prospect of moving then. I had basically already told Shrewsbury that I was leaving. Nothing happened, though, in terms of another club coming in for me and I began pre-season training with Shrewsbury in July. It wasn't like it is today. There was no freedom of contract as such. This was the pre-Bosman era. So although I had said that I wouldn't sign again for Shrewsbury, they retained my registration, although I was free to negotiate with whoever I want, and they were holding out for a good-sized transfer fee. It wasn't all bad though as the other side of the coin was that they had to keep paying me. I suppose technically I wasn't within my rights to talk to Stoke before the end of the previous season, but it was common knowledge I was going.

But then, just when I thought the move was sorted out in August, everything changed at the very last minute. I was just leaving the car park at Shrewsbury after training when I had a knock on the window of my car. It was Graham Turner, and he said, "How do you fancy going to Everton?" Now they were a very big club – still are obviously – and I went up there to talk to the manager, and it looked like that move would go ahead, but I failed the medical.

What happened there was that Everton looked into my history and two years earlier I'd had a back problem. I'd had a small stress fracture in my back, which had actually healed, but their medical advice was not to take the risk as it could cause me to break down. So Durban came back in and it took a couple of weeks to get everything sorted out, but eventually, right at the start of September 1980, I finally signed for Stoke.

The fee was over £250,000, a lot of money in those days, when there had only been a couple of £1m transfers, but it didn't bring me any pressure. I thought I was worth it! I was at the top of my form and I showed that on my home debut.

YOU HAVE TO prove yourself when you sign for a new club. Stoke had started the season abominably. They'd just been spanked 5-0 at Nottingham Forest, having already lost 5-1 at Norwich on the opening day. Young central defender Dave McAughtrie made his debut at the City Ground because of an injury crisis with Doyle, Smith and O'Callaghan all injured. That defeat at Forest left Stoke bottom of the table, so the only way was up. There was a lot of apprehension around because of the start they'd made and the injuries. In fact I remember the injury crisis was so acute that the manager cancelled a practice match on the Tuesday of my first week due to a lack of fit players as Adrian Heath, Ray Evans and Peter Hampton were also struggling.

In fact my actual debut was in a League Cup second round second leg tie at Manchester City in midweek. Paul Richardson played centre-half alongside Denis Thorley, so it must have been one of Stoke's least experienced defensive partnerships ever. Not surprisingly we lost 3-0 to go out 4-1 on aggregate, but I was looking forward to playing at home. Stoke and Shrewsbury hadn't agreed a fee for me, so it was decided by a transfer tribunal on the Friday before the Leeds game and it was set at £262,000

I will always consider that match against Leeds as my real debut. Mike Doyle was fit enough to play, so Dave McAughtrie was dropped after his nightmare against Forest. We began that game absolutely on fire. Loek Ursem, who was a very underrated player, had a shot touched over for a corner and from that kick, which I took, the ball was half-cleared to the edge of the box, where Ursem launched into an overhead kick that sailed into the far corner of the net. A great start.

We really pummelled them then. Lee Chapman raced on to a through ball, but Lukic just got there to foil him. Paul Bracewell was winning everything tigerishly in midfield and I was finding plenty of space on the wing.

Then we got a free kick about 25 yards out on the left hand side. I'd always taken the free kicks at Shrewsbury, in fact I took all the set pieces, and I grabbed the ball and said, "I'll have it," No one challenged me. It didn't seem as if anyone else wanted it. So I put the ball down and took the free kick. John Lukic, who went on to be a fantastic goalkeeper for both Leeds and Arsenal, was in goal and I left him helpless as my shot flew into the far right hand corner of the net. A 25-yarder in the top corner, on your home debut, that was great, you know. It was a nice way to say, "hello" and it got me instant recognition.

I used to class myself as an old-fashioned inside-forward. I could shoot with both feet, pass with both feet and head it reasonably well. The only thing I couldn't do was tackle, I couldn't tackle for toffee, but that was someone else's job. I could take people on, get to the byline and cross. I think my versatility meant that I could play anywhere, which allowed Alan Durban and then Richie Barker to use me in a variety of positions.

I was reasonably accurate from a dead ball and that's why I became the set-piece taker.

Of course everyone remembers the near post corner routine, which came a bit later on in my Stoke career and it proved to be a very effective tactic for us. We scored a lot of goals from it. It was the result of a tremendous amount of practice. We had Brendan or George, the big lads, at the near post flicking the ball on for other players to run on to. It was very difficult to defend against and it scared a lot of people and sides didn't want to give corners away against us. In fact our fans used to cheer corners like we had actually scored a goal!

It mystifies me why it isn't used these days. In fact you rarely see sides scoring from corner kicks any more. You constantly see people swinging in a high-paced corner, which the keeper catches or they fail to get the ball past the first defender. The beauty of our near post corner was that, because it was curling in to that area, if a defender won it he would have to put it out for another corner. And the goalkeeper is kept out of the game as he can't get through the bodies to get to the ball. It was also a very effective pressure tactic. I remember we played West Ham at home one night and we must have had six or seven corners in a row, and there was a tremendous sense of anticipation that we would score because we were putting them under so much pressure.

THAT DAY AGAINST Leeds, they were struggling. I remember setting the crowd roaring by beating Brian Greenhoff time after time. I put Ursem in for another shot, but Lukic parried and Paul Bracewell hit the bar after chasing down a long through ball and lobbing Lukic. We were all over them to be honest.

Then I forced successive corners and from the second I played a short ball to Peter Hampton. His cross found Inchy Heath, who controlled it and drove the ball left-footed on the half-volley into the net. 3-0 before half-time was a dream. We were absolutely cruising it.

At half-time I remember looking round the dressing room. We'd played so well and we were all obviously thinking, "Yes. This is a team." We couldn't wait to get out for the second half. The game was effectively over and the second half was just exhibition stuff.

The only thing I remember from the second half was Leeds fans constantly chanting, "Adamson Out!" and they held up play by keeping the ball when it went amongst them.

They also had Paul Madeley stretchered off and then Greenhoff needed smelling salts to recover from another tackle! The game petered out a bit with Leeds having a couple of chances, but Foxy dealt with them well, making one flying save from Flynn.

It was a spectacular start for this new team and everyone was excited about the possibilities of this side. We thought that we'd really stumbled on to something. It was over in a flash and I'll never forget the buzz and the reaction I got from fans afterwards. I felt fantastic and I felt as though I had arrived and I was looking forward to a successful season. It really made it for me when the headline that night in the *Sentinel* was 'Maguire Fires Rampant City'.

FANTASTIC THOUGH THAT day was, the next weeks were tinged with a problem, which caused me so much trouble it's untrue. As part of my medical to join Stoke they had injected a dye into my back to see if it travelled somewhere it wasn't supposed to. I had to undergo these tests because SW Taylor's, the insurance people, wouldn't insure me unless they knew the old back injury was OK.

That dye reacted with my metabolism. I felt a burning sensation in my back and by the time I played at Arsenal on the Saturday my back was on fire and then by the Monday morning I was in bits. I then had to spend six weeks in a plaster cast and that set me back physically and it seriously affected my confidence. I think the dye was made by Glaxo and subsequently I found out that some people had been crippled for life as a result of this dye, so when I look back I think I got away quite lightly.

I was never quite right after that for the rest of that season and I think it seriously affected how the fans thought about me. I had made such an impact that day against Leeds and that was the real me. What they saw for the rest of the season wasn't. I had played so well against Leeds and felt on top of the world, so there was lots of hype about when I was coming back. And I didn't play until the FA Cup replay against Wolves in January. But I wasn't really fit and I was way below the pace, but Durban had asked me to play, so I did. I hadn't even played a reserve team match. I lost a lot of credibility because of that. We kept the full extent of my problem within the club so fans weren't aware of what was going on, so they thought they'd signed a lemon – even though they'd seen what I could do on my debut. It was just a quirk of fate that the reaction had occurred.

ALAN DURBAN LEAVING at the end of that season was probably the worst thing that happened not just for me personally, but also for the club. He'd built a great team and everyone was looking forward to having a good season, but we went away to Barbados for a pre-season tour and out there he broke the news that he was going to Sunderland and it just flattened us really. I will never, ever understand why Durban was allowed to leave. I know he was offered big money to go and turn Sunderland around, but Stoke didn't seem to make him a counter offer to try and keep him.

Of course then all the young players began to go. Chapman, Heath and Bracewell all left, mainly because they weren't appreciated by Durban's replacement at Stoke, the man who had been his assistant at Shrewsbury, Richie Barker. They had been perfectly happy under Durban, but all of a sudden they were gone and Richie was signing players on the downward slope of their careers. For me Barker was the wrong guy in the wrong place with the wrong people. I was surprised they didn't go for someone like Howard Kendall. He'd been player-coach, but had gone to manage Blackburn as he wanted to be his own man. He ended up signing Heath and Bracewell once he went to Everton, of course, and they won everything together at Goodison Park. Lee Chapman left too and he'd been scoring 20 goals a season. How do you replace that? Well, we didn't.

IT DIDN'T HELP that Barker had chosen to play the long ball game in the summer of 1983. That was just horrendous. Football wasn't fun and it drove a lot of talented players away. The problems that all created meant we started the 1983/84 season horribly. At Christmas we and Wolves were so far adrift of the rest of the division we were effectively down and out. But then Barker was sacked and Bill Asprey took over. He consulted Tony Waddington about whether he thought bringing Alan Hudson back was a good idea – Huddy had been playing in America in the summer and then in Chelsea's reserves for the British season. Waddo recommended he do it and Huddy came in, met us on that plane and transformed the season.

We actually only had 17 points after 24 games and had just been hammered 6-0 at Queens Park Rangers on that horrible plastic pitch they had. Then Huddy arrived and we went on this incredible run which saw us pick up 33 points in the remaining 18 games. That's Championship form; at least, certainly, Europe. We beat teams like Liverpool, Arsenal, Ipswich, Coventry and Luton. We played fantastic football and somehow dragged ourselves into a position where we could save ourselves on the final day of the season if we beat Wolves, who had not had such a renaissance and had been down for weeks, and one other result of the four other teams in contention for the drop went our way.

We'd won at Luton on Bank Holiday Monday, when Ian Painter scored a real striker's goal, lashing home a loose ball in the box. We'd had to win all those games otherwise we were dead. It wasn't an option not to. But we could do that because Alan had come and changed the atmosphere at the club. The results began to come and we got our pride back and we were having fun doing what we were doing. As we collected points, we thought, "hold on a second, we can do this." It was a complete change of culture and you have to give credit to Bill for bringing him in.

WE KNEW WE had to win. But we could still win and go down if we didn't win by enough goals. Wolves were a dispirited side, so the fixtures worked out very well for us in that sense. We felt confident we'd win that game, but it was all about what we did in relation to others.

It turned out to be a great day for me as I bagged four goals. The first one was a header at the back post. The second was an overhead kick from around the penalty spot. Huddy crossed it and I went for it and it flew in; sometimes things just go for you. Then I got a penalty as well and by the time it got to ten minutes from the end we were winning 3-0. But there was Bill Asprey on the touchline shouting and gesticulating that we needed another one. We needed to win by four. I remember thinking, "I've scored a hat-trick, we are winning 3-0, it's the last day of the season and we are still going down!"

Sammy McIlroy had gone down for the first penalty we had, which completed my hat-trick, but then, in the last minute of the game, Alan Dodd brought me down for another spot-kick - and there were rumours about that. Doddy had played for ten years at

Stoke and he loved the club. Everyone knew that and he'd only really left because he'd become dissatisfied with Barker just like all the others that had left like Mickey Thomas and Paul Bracewell. So, being a true Stokie, people said that he knew we needed another goal and he'd tripped me deliberately! I don't know what the truth is. I think it may well be a sort of myth that has developed and all the uncertainty adds to that myth. It certainly never crossed my mind at the time, but I was sure he'd fouled me. I got up to crack home my fourth goal, and the goal which we now all thought had saved the club. It was one hell of a release.

What people tend to forget is that I missed a sitter to make it five. Sammy McIlroy got to the byline and chipped it to the far post and I dived to head the ball towards goal and as I did so I took cramp in my calves. It was a hot day and we'd put everything we had into the game. That kept me from putting the full power on it and the ball drifted across and hit the outside of the far post. Now that would have been something – scoring five. Not many people have done that for Stoke. Mind you not many have scored four to be honest!

THE CELEBRATIONS WERE fantastic. I got carried around the pitch shoulder-high with everyone shouting and cheering. It was wonderful. We knew we'd survived, but we didn't really know what had gone on elsewhere. It wasn't until we got back into the dressing room that we realised the number of goals we scored was immaterial! I don't know where Bill had got it from that we needed four, but it certainly spurred us on.

In the event Birmingham had drawn 0-0, so we finished two points ahead of them. We had been as dead as you could get, so it was an unbelievable escape.

I think there must have been over 100,000 Stoke fans at the match, because everyone I meet says, "Oh yes, I was at that game, I was at that game." It's amazing how many people say they were there!

The reason I haven't selected that game, though, is because of what happened next. Don't get me wrong, the Wolves game was a massive game, but during the following week it was effectively made clear to me that the club didn't want me. I was on the transfer list already and hadn't played a lot of games, mostly coming on as substitute. My career wasn't going anywhere and my contract was up in the summer. So the club made me an offer, which I didn't think was worth my while accepting. It was their prerogative and I got an offer to go abroad on a far better deal. I wanted to stay at Stoke because the resurgence had given me belief that the club could go places again, but I decided to accept the offer from Tacoma Stars, near Seattle, to play in the American Indoor Soccer League. The money was very good, but I broke my leg out there and I decided that it wasn't the best career move so I came back and played for the Vale, where I helped them win promotion during my three years there.

So that Wolves game, though a great day, is always tinged with the sadness of knowing it was my last game for Stoke and I prefer to remember the day I joined and the feeling I got from my debut, which was a sparkling team performance, as well as probably my best game in a Stoke shirt.

MARK CHAMBERLAIN: BORN 19 NOVEMBER 1961, STOKE; 125 GAMES, 18 GOALS

Mark Chamberlain

Birmingham City 1 Stoke City 4

League Division One

Saturday 4 September 1982

I WAS SPEAKING to my son the other day and I realised that this game at Birmingham was not only the day I scored my first Stoke goal, but also one of only two occasions I scored two goals for Stoke. In fact I thought I scored three goals, but I had one taken away from me that should have been mine. I never did score a hat-trick in my career, so that would have made it even more special than it was. Even so, I thought this game was probably the best I played in my career and that's why I've chosen it.

THIS MATCH ROUNDED off an incredible start to my first week at Stoke. The weird thing is that I nearly didn't join the club. I was happy at Port Vale, where I had started my career and was playing in a good little team with players like Kenny Beech, Phil Sproson, Russell Bromage and, of course, my brother Neville up front. John McGrath was the manager at the time and he called me aside one day just before the 1982/83 season was due to start and told me that Stoke manager Richie Barker was coming down to the ground to talk to me and also goalkeeper Mark Harrison. John then told me what wages to ask for!

So Richie sat me down and said that Stoke wanted to sign me and that he would pay me exactly the figure that John McGrath had told me to ask for. So I thought, 'These two have been talking!' and at first I refused to sign. I thought they were conspiring to make sure I didn't ask for the earth, so the move would go ahead;

on Stoke's part, because they wanted to keep the wages down and on Vale's part because they wanted the money from the transfer fee. I think that was a bit of a shock for Richie. For a Fourth Division player to say that to a First Division manager was unheard of I think! It was actually the first and probably the last time I ever spoke up for myself during my career.

John McGrath came back in to the room and said, "What are you doing? You are going to mess the deal up if you go on like this." Now this was in the days way before agents, so I had to ask for what I was worth. But we got it sorted out and I signed just two days before the start of the season. I was happy as Larry to be at Stoke and looking forward to playing in the First Division.

I'll never forget speaking to Richie Barker on the pitch at the Victoria Ground the following day when he said, "We're playing Arsenal tomorrow. Where do you want to play?"

And I thought, 'You're the manager. Where do you want me to play?'

"Where do you want to play? You can play wherever you want."

He couldn't decide if I should play up front, where I had played a lot of my time for Vale in the Fourth Division, or wide on the right, which was actually my favoured position. He was umm-ing and aah-ing so eventually I said, "Look. I think I'll play wide on the right." It was probably because I felt a bit more comfortable on the wing and I had spent the time at Vale switching between the two positions because of necessity and I was never a natural goalscorer. That was the moment when I became a winger for ten years. And, as they say, the rest is history!

The thing I didn't fully realise was that Arsenal's left-back was the England left-back Kenny Sansom. He was very experienced and had just had an extremely good World Cup finals in Spain, in which England had only conceded one goal in five games and had only gone out in a strange kind of second group stage, which involved three teams, only one of which qualified for the semi-finals. England drew both of their games 0-0 and because West Germany defeated Spain 2-1 in the other match, England went out without losing a game.

So Kenny was this incredible player that should, in theory, not have given a Fourth Division player like me a kick, but I had something of a dream debut against him. I suppose that match was another that was in contention for my favourite game. It was daunting enough to be playing Arsenal and I had always thought as a Fourth Division player that I was a million miles away from England internationals and now here I was facing one.

What I really remember about that day is the atmosphere at the Vic. The Boothen End was in full cry, as it always was when we were playing well. For me only two kops were better in the country – Everton and Liverpool – and then only because they were bigger and had more people standing on them. I used to read all those annuals when I was a kid and dream about playing in these incredible stadia which held 30, 40, 50,000 people. I'd never really heard or felt anything like it before. Playing in the Fourth Division you don't really experience anything like that. Vale Park had these big open spaces and only about 3,000 people in it, which didn't generate any atmosphere at all.

My debut had this bit of added spice to it because Lee Chapman was making his debut for Arsenal, having just moved from Stoke. Obviously I hadn't known Lee, but I think he'd said one or two things about Stoke and some of the players he'd left behind, so there was a considerable edge amongst the lads to show him that he'd been wrong to leave.

I actually don't think I played quite as well as some people now seem to remember, but I think it was quite exciting for people when I started to go past Sansom. I don't think Stoke fans had seen someone like me playing against a big team. The game at the time in England had done away with wingers mostly and also it was unusual for a team like Stoke to be taking the game to a team like Arsenal. Normally little clubs tried to just defend against the big boys. That was the prevailing thinking. But in signing myself and Mickey Thomas just before the start of that season, Richie Barker had stumbled across a side who played good, flowing, passing football and it all just clicked on that opening day.

It couldn't have started any better when I skipped past Sansom after five minutes and crossed perfectly on to the head of George

Berry for the opening goal. Lee Chapman got himself booked early on, which curbed his effectiveness because he couldn't put himself about so physically any more and Georgie Berry basically snuffed him out. Brendan O'Callaghan headed home another of my crosses to make it 2-0, and despite them pulling a goal back through Alan Sunderland, we won comfortably. It was a great way to make my debut. I contrasted fairly markedly with the debut Mark Harrison, who had been the other half of the transfer deal from Vale made that same day in the reserves. Mark broke his jaw and had to be on a liquid diet for a month! Fortunately he got better quickly and was fit enough to be available when Peter Fox got himself sent off against Luton to come into the team and put in some great performances.

I was shattered at the end of the Arsenal game. I remember I did do well, but maybe it was the impact that I made that causes people to remember that game so much, as I think I had much better ones later.

ALL SEASON LONG I destroyed full-backs for fun. It wasn't actually anything new for me because I'd been doing it for Vale, but to be taking apart all these top division full-backs was very pleasing. In those days full-backs were good footballers rather than quick players and so when we played Man City, for example, on the Tuesday after that opening game, they had a player called Bobby McDonald at left-back. He was a good footballer, but not quick and I murdered him. The only problem was that, although Big Bren kept nodding down my crosses there was no one there to finish them off. Barker had started with a player called Peter Griffiths, who was really a left-sided midfielder, up front with Bren and it didn't come off. So somehow we lost that match 1-0. I was determined to make up for that in the next game, on the following Saturday at Birmingham.

The Birmingham game was a very special match for me. I gave their left-back, Phil Hawker, a bit of a roasting. All day long I had players trying to mark me tightly. I remember Hawker and Kevan Broadhurst double-teaming me for a lot of the first half, but I kept running at them with the ball.

Early on I created a chance, but chipped just over the bar. Next time the ball came to me I swerved inside the pair of them and knocked it on to sprint on to. In chasing down the ball, Hawker just beat me to it and tried a floated back pass to their keeper, Jim Blyth. But the ball beat the keeper and rolled in.

Then I scored a good, good goal. I picked the ball up on the halfway line after it was cleared from a corner we were defending and the two centre-halves, van den Hauwe and Scott, came to me and I beat them both then setting off for goal. Hawker came across from his full-back position, but I beat him halfway inside their half and there was a midfielder haring back as well, but my pace carried me clear of him as I raced towards goal. I beat the keeper and slotted the ball home after running probably 50 yards. It was a great goal if I say so myself, but it was something I have always had the ability to do. All the time I had been at Vale I had tried to take people on and cause them problems. I was just lucky I suppose that this happened in a First Division game.

Within a couple of minutes I'd got another goal to add to the collection. This one was very different and had a whiff of controversy about it – amongst our team anyway. From a corner, I somehow looped a header towards goal. My heading was never the best, but when I got it right, it often worked well. It hit the woodwork and seemed to go over the line from where I was standing, but Dave McAughtrie, our central defender finished it off to make sure. When we got back to the dressing room at half-time he was trying to claim he'd scored, but I wasn't having that. I finally got that one after a bit of an argument! It was definitely over the line already.

Frustration set in for Birmingham then. Their midfielder Kevin Dillon, who had something of a reputation, upended me and then took a second kick at me while I was lying on the floor and the ref sent him off. Apparently he'd actually only just come back from suspension. Birmingham had a fairly tough team at the time and once they realised they were being taken apart, some pretty nasty challenges came flying in. Dillon had lost it a bit before that and had begun trying to kick me out of the game. The good thing was I was too quick for him to catch me most of the time.

Now we were playing ten men and soon it was 4-0. Now this was the goal that I still claim completed my hat-trick. I hit this driven volley from the edge of the box that rebounded down off the bar and Peter Griffiths finished it off. I still think that it went straight in, so I'd like to claim a hat-trick. Officially. Change the record books! Of course with no TV there to record the game we'll never know for sure. A hat-trick would have been fantastic.

IT'S A GOOD job we had something to discuss a half-time – like who'd scored which goal - because Richie Barker was at a loss for words. I don't think he'd ever seen anything like the football we were playing. Not only was I playing probably the best game of my life, the whole side were cruising. George Berry dominated at the back, while Sammy McIlroy and Paul Bracewell ran midfield.

Everything went well for us that day. Even in the second half when Foxy was rounded by Van Mierlo, the ball rolled loose to Mick Harford, who shot wide of the empty net. When they did finally score with ten minutes to go - thanks to Alan Curbishley's low shot - it was way, way too late to bother us. It was a great win for Stoke and really served notice that we were going to be a threat in the First Division that season. The reporter of from the *Sentinel* must have enjoyed it because his headline was 'A Touch of Genius'!

MY FIRST GOAL was a special, special goal and I still remember it vividly 25 years later. It actually hurts me that there were no TV cameras at the ground. In those days only about three or four games each weekend were covered by TV and there was no one at Birmingham with a camera that day, so it's a good job I can remember it clear as day because there's no video to remind me. I can't show it to my son, either, so he has to listen to his old man telling him how he ran from the half-way line and beat five players to score a goal just like Thierry Henry – in fact when I'm telling the story I'm better than Henry. Does he believe me? What do you think!

I sometimes look at the Stoke City website to see if someone has magically discovered any archive footage in the vaults at the BBC or Central TV, but I don't think there is anything from that game. I wish there was.

And of course the other difference is that back then, even if the game was on TV, if you were on ITV, it would only be shown in the Central area, not nationally, and certainly not across the whole world as Premiership football is now. Imagine how many people would have seen that goal if I had scored it today; everyone from Thailand to Canada, South Africa to Brazil. It wasn't just me that missed out, of course, lots of boys were doing incredible things every single weekend, but if you got lucky and did it in front of the cameras it could change your career.

Remember Hoddle's chipped goal for Spurs against Watford? That was on Match of the Day, and it made him into this mystical genius of a player. Don't get me wrong, it was fantastic, but, it's just because Spurs were fashionable and on TV a lot that Hoddle's goal was recorded for posterity and replayed time and time again.

While I'm on the subject, TV didn't help me in my career at all. My performances for Stoke forced me into the new England manager Bobby Robson's squad and I came on as a substitute to win my first cap against Luxembourg in 1982. At the end of the season England went on tour to South America. We played Brazil in the Maracana and Robson at the time was experimenting with playing both myself and John Barnes as out-and-out wingers. It was very exciting to play in that team as we had a great centre-forward in Mark Hateley up front to get on to our crosses. Anyway I had a great game in the first half against Brazil and tore my full-back to shreds. He had a nightmare and I thought I'd done brilliantly. What I didn't know was that the satellite which was beaming the game back to fans in England had gone down and so no one ever saw the first half of that game. They managed to get it back working at half-time and so coverage began then. As it happened John Barnes put on an absolutely electrifying show as we won 2-0 to register the first, and so far only, victory for an England team over Brazil on their turf. He scored that wonderful goal which, yes, gets repeated over and over again even today. It made him a global superstar. In fact as he was running through swathes of gold-shirted defenders, I was shouting for Barnesy to pass it to me as I was in the clear, but he was head down and go and he beat the keeper to score with his right foot. To be fair to John, it was a fantastic goal and for five or six seasons after that, especially after he moved to Liverpool, he was the best player in the country.

ON MY DEBUT against Luxembourg I scored with a header. It was an easy game and we were winning comfortably and would eventually run out 9-0 winners. It was unusual enough for me to score from a header, but it was also from the side I can't really head from. Unfortunately I am a right-winger, but I head better from the ball coming over from the right wing, when really I am only going to get on the end of a cross from the left. But that goal was actually used in the FA training manual as the perfect example of how to perform a downward header. I was so chuffed with that as I was hardly a renowned header of the ball; all the more so that I actually headed it with my nose! This is where TV doesn't help me again because if you look closely at the pictures from that game the goal goes in on a wide shot and looks fantastic, but when it cuts to a close up of me celebrating and then running back to the halfway line I am actually rubbing my nose! A tell-tale giveaway!!

I'd played for England schoolboys at Wembley twice, but it was fantastic to play there with the place full. Robson's team was very exciting and I enjoyed it. I felt comfortable in the company of these better players like Bryan Robson, Glenn Hoddle, Terry Butcher, Peter Shilton and I thought I was worthy of my place in the squad.

I had a bad game in the last match of that summer tour of South America against Chile. We lost 2-0 and everyone had a stinker to be fair. But then I got injured, which I did quite a lot, and I was dropped from the squad. Around that time Robson decided to go with one winger and John was the man in possession. I never felt I was any worse player than I had been three months previously. Things just didn't quite work for me in the end with England. I used to have a go at that bloody Mick Duxbury who played at right-back. I used to be shouting at him, "Give me the ball." But he always used to pass it inside to Bryan Robson, who was his team-mate and captain at Manchester United. Time and time again. He just wouldn't give it to me and that really didn't help either. It was a big problem for me and he was a pain in the butt.

I DID PICK up a lot of injuries and my hamstrings were the main problem. I had a bad hamstring just like Michael Owen has now. Those of us who are quick players have these fast twitch muscles that allow us to run just that bit quicker, but they are more vulnerable. It didn't help of course that my preparation for games was just a bit of gym work and have a little warm up. The techniques for warming up are so much better these days and I was forced back into playing before I was quite ready. So I had two years when I wasn't quite right. Football has moved on quite a lot now and a lot less is left to chance, although they are still getting injuries these days, so it's not quite as scientific as they'd have you believe. The beauty of the squad system now is that if you are injured they don't rush you back so you're not playing on old injuries or with cortisone injections all the time.

What has changed, though, is people like Sammy McIlroy who used to come in 20 minutes or so before kick-off as he'd been in the lounge looking at his horses! He'd just get changed quick, put his kit on, walk out and play fantastic. You won't get that these days!

We had a fantastic midfield at Stoke; Bracewell, McIlroy, Thomas and myself. The way I wanted to play was enhanced by them getting the ball to me early and in on-on-one situations. For me Paul Bracewell was a very underrated player and Big Brendan was fantastic too as he would knock the ball down and it would drop for me to run on to. I also had Derek Parkin just behind me at full-back and he was fantastic.

Foxy was a great, great goalkeeper, especially for his height. He was only 5ft 10in or 11in. I don't think he would get a game these days, would he? You have to be 6ft 6in and be able to kick the ball to the other penalty box. He used to always come in early and warm up and do weights with myself and Brendan O'Callaghan. He was a lovely character. I went and played for him when he was manager at Exeter for the last 18 months of my career and that was great fun.

It was always either Brendan O'Callaghan or George Berry who always seemed to get on to the end of my crosses. In the incredible game against Luton – another match that I almost picked – George somehow managed to anticipate a cross from me, when even I didn't think I'd get it into the box. I'd got my back to goal by the goal-line and managed to swivel and dink it in to the near post, where George had run and dived to head home. We had a kind of telepathy between us. He could read what I was going to do.

Of course he was also used in the famous short corner routine that got us so many goals. He used to claim that he'd grown his hair into that Afro he had purely as a tactic to ensure the defenders and goalkeeper standing behind him couldn't see the ball coming, so he could flick it on at the near post! George also claimed his haircut was a fashion statement. I think it was either a fashion statement or he was too lazy to cut it. Mind you, being from Wolverhampton I can believe it with that fashion sense! Quite often he'd turn up for training with his Afro comb stuck in his hair.

THAT FIRST SEASON at Stoke was fantastic. I view it as probably the best time of my career, although it's pushed hard by the second half of the following season when Alan Hudson came and we somehow dragged ourselves clear of relegation.

I don't like to talk about the 1984/85 season. It was a tough season, because we just had a bunch of kids in the side, although I was gutted when Sunderland broke our record for the lowest top flight points total in 2005/06. I was telling everyone during the run in to that season how I hoped they didn't break it as that was the only record I had on the books!

Once we'd been relegated it was inevitable that I would be sold to balance the books. I had an agent at the time and he said that Chelsea were in for me and I had a choice between them or Sheffield Wednesday, who were managed by the infamous Howard Wilkinson. But the Chelsea deal didn't come off and Wednesday came back in for me a couple of months into the new season. I actually didn't want to go, but Stoke said that I had to as the club desperately needed the money. The fee was set by tribunal at just £300,000, which gutted the club. I think Chrissie Waddle had just gone from Newcastle to Tottenham for £900,00 and so Stoke were holding out for £600,00 for me as I was the best right-winger in the country by a mile.

I actually knew that Wednesday weren't the club for me before I signed because I had heard of Howard's reputation, but I had to go as in those days you didn't really get much say in the matter. As soon as I signed I got into training and the right back there was a guy called Mel Sterland, who was a very funny fellow. In the very first practice game we played together, I was losing my full-back and Mel shouted, "Spin" and belted a long ball down the wing for me to chase. Well, I'd come short to pick the ball up off him, turn and run at the full-back as I always liked to do. Anyway he kept doing this all session and afterwards I said to him, "What are you doing? Just give me the ball short."

"I can't do that," he said. "I have to shout 'spin' and belt the ball down the line into the space for you. It's your job to get it!" He was laughing as he said it as he knew that was totally alien to me.

Playing for Howard Wilkinson, how shall I say, wasn't for me. I think there was one occasion when we were playing Arsenal away and the team was packed full of big lads, who all kept running all day. I was selected as the substitute – there was only one in those days. I wasn't happy at not playing and was sitting there grumpily on the bench when Peter Eustace, the coach, came and sat down next to me.

"You don't look very happy," he said.

"I'm not. I'm only sub."

"Oh, you've done well to be sub in this team, son," he said. He was obviously surprised that Wilkinson had selected me at all. In fact I'm surprised he bothered signing me! Howard tried to reinvent me as something else, although I'm not sure what, but I was simply an out-and-out winger. He didn't want to use players that could play a bit like myself and David Hirst, who went on to become a Wednesday legend, or even Siggy Jonsson, who was a fantastic player and went on to do well at Arsenal. The three of us had all the talent and pace, but he wouldn't play us because we wanted to do something different when we had the ball rather than play to his pattern. Howard's football was horrible and it's almost dead now thankfully.

It surprised me that he went on to set up the FA's structure for youngsters to play football as his teams never played football! I was surprised that Leeds won the Championship with him as manager, but when I saw Mel Sterland again after that, he told me that Eric Cantona and Gordon Strachan hadn't listened to a word Wilkinson had said. They'd just got on with playing their own game and won the league for Leeds.

So it was a long few years at Wednesday and I was glad to get away. I had a few seasons at Portsmouth, which was a bit bleak, and then moved to Brighton and latterly Exeter. Brighton was a nightmare as the manager was Liam Brady. He's found his role now as Academy Director at Arsenal, although I didn't think his coaching methods were too brilliant. We had some good players in Steve Foster, Colin Pates and Dean Wilkins. But I felt the young lads in the squad weren't being taught the game properly. It showed as Brady didn't last very long.

I went on to play until I was 35 and played over 500 league games. I had the opportunity to go into coaching at Portsmouth when Jim Smith offered me a job when I was 32, but I wanted to play on and enjoy my last few seasons, rather than to pack in and coach at that age. So, after a spell as manager at Fareham Town in the Southern League, now I work in Southampton on behalf of the football club in the community here with underprivileged kids, helping them to learn skills for life by enjoying football and other sports such as tennis, volleyball and rugby to help broaden their horizons. Most of them are a nightmare, but they all seem to focus and do well when they are with us. The problems start when they are being influenced by their peers or have unstable home lives and then we have to pick up the pieces. It's challenging and rewarding and I really enjoy the work.

WHEREVER I WENT I never found football as good as in that first season at Stoke. We really played some superb stuff. For excitement and achieving things that was the best time of my career. It's incredible to think I'd actually only been at Stoke for nine days when we played that game at Birmingham. But I still think I scored a hat-trick at St. Andrews.

PETER FOX: BORN 5 JULY 1957, SCUNTHORPE; 478 GAMES, 0 GOALS

Peter Fox

Stoke City 4 Luton Town 4

League Division One

Saturday 25 September 1982

YOU MAY THINK it strange, but I have chosen a game in which I actually only played about 25 minutes. To be honest it's not my favourite game as such, but it is a game for which I am remembered and one which should be remembered because it had absolutely everything. It was one hell of a game. But why on earth would I pick a game in which I only played less than half an hour?

Well I remember Brian Clough did a series on Central TV just after he retired called *Brian Clough's Favourites*, in which he picked his top ten football matches of all time and that was one of them. And if it was good enough for Cloughie, then it's certainly good enough for me.

IT WAS ALL Dave Watson's fault. I would say that wouldn't I! But it was, it really was, when I think back and relive what happened. We had a free kick on the halfway line. We were leading 2-1 against a Luton side that were one of the most entertaining footballing sides in the country. We'd also started the season with a huge bang thanks to the introduction of Mark Chamberlain and Mickey Thomas to the starting line-up. This was only the seventh game we'd played with this now legendary line-up and we'd won four of the six so far, scoring 13 goals in the process and we were sitting pretty in fourth place in the table.

So we had this free kick and Dave Watson took it. Dave was a very experienced England international centre-half, who was a consummate professional. He'd made his name at Manchester

City and won ?? England caps, but on this occasion he tried to take the free kick too quickly and only succeeded in playing it straight against the referee, who had no chance of getting out of the way. The ball fell to a Luton midfielder who helped it on over Dave's head for Paul Walsh to run on to. I was on the edge of my area ready to sweep up as I always was and I saw Paul momentarily think to himself that he wasn't going to get to the ball before me. He slightly stopped his run and that caused me to think that I had time to be a bit clever and allow the ball to run back into my area so I could pick it up, rather than having to go outside the box and clear it with my foot. But I misjudged it a little bit as the ball didn't quite have as much on it as both I and Walshy thought. He realised it a split second before me, though, and accelerated again and I ended up caught in no man's land having to try to dive on the ball just outside the area as he challenged me for it. I went down on to it trying to keep my arms out of the way by holding them tightly by my sides and sticking my chest out. But the ball squeezed out from under me and Paul nipped around me and scored.

At least that's what we both thought had happened. The referee was a bloke called Gilbert Napthine. His whistle went and I thought that he'd given the goal, but the next thing I know is that there are confrontations going on all round me. It was funny when I think back about it. Four or five of their players were surrounding the ref wanting me to be sent off, while Walshy was trying to tell them to shut up because he wanted the goal! I remember him shouting, "I scored, I scored, I want the goal!" It is quite amazing to watch the video of the game back on TV and see it all going off.

I was about to become the very first victim of a new law which had been introduced at the start of the season that said that goalkeepers who handled the ball outside the penalty area must be sent off. Because this law was new it was at the forefront of everyone's mind, particularly the ref. He called me over and simply pointed to the dressing room. He never said a word to me. And cards weren't in use at the time, so there was no red card to be dramatically brandished in my direction with a flourish á la David Beckham against Argentina in the World Cup in France in 1998.

I only got sent off on one other occasion in my career. It was while playing for Exeter and I deliberately brought down an opposing forward when he was bearing down on goal. Now that was precisely what the law was designed to punish. A guy called Alfie Buksh was the referee on that occasion and he ran over to me as I picked myself up and said, ever so politely, "Mr Fox. I am sending you off for a deliberate foul."

And I thought, 'Yeah. You're right'!

I could understand that one, but the sending off against Luton I still can't really fathom. I will never forget Gilbert Napthine. These days, of course, you only get sent off for denying an obvious goalscoring opportunity with a handball. If you just step outside holding the ball by accident you just get booked. What I did was not a professional foul, it was just a misjudgement by about a foot. People had been waiting for an incident and a referee to be brave enough to administer the law and it just so happened it was me, but the incident was actually used for a long time as an example to referees as to how not to apply the law! Just my luck.

Of course now everyone's used to all the sendings off. They are ten a penny and if you get through a season as a keeper without being sent off you have done very well. Back then you'd pretty much have to assault or commit GBH against someone to get yourself sent off as a goalkeeper. That's what I'd been used to. Often, even if you did something, as long as you looked remorseful you got away with it because keepers had this unwritten special protection, but the law change had stopped all that and this was the moment that I realised it!

What annoyed me even more was that later that season both Gary Bailey at Manchester United and Ray Clemence at Liverpool did exactly the same thing, very similar situations to myself and didn't get sent off. So I suppose I was the guinea pig in a sense.

TO SAY I was crestfallen would be something of an understatement. It was heartbreaking for me. One of the worst things was having to go and sit alone in the dressing rooms for the rest of the game. Now there were only tiny little windows in the top of the home changing rooms at the Vic, but in the toilets there were slightly bigger ones that looked out on to the pitch and you could open those windows, so I spent the remainder of the game with a fairly restricted view of the corners of the pitch, trying to keep up with the incredible events that were occurring out there. It was a slightly unusual view to say the least.

Watching the whole thing unfold was amazing. It was the kind of game which seemed as if it had a Hollywood script written for it with incredible plot twists and ridiculous turnabouts that would have graced any blockbuster film! I still feel privileged to have played a part in it, even if it was only a short one.

I like to think that my role in the whole saga was integral to the way the drama unfolded.

Both teams had been playing well and scoring goals early in the season, and it had continued in the first half hour. Nine times out of ten when you get two sides as good as those Stoke and Luton teams playing each other you get a nil-niller, but that wasn't the case that day. The game had already been an absolute stormer.

We had Mark Chamberlain, Mickey Thomas, Sammy McIlroy and Paul Maguire causing havoc, while they had Paul Walsh, David Moss, Brian Stein and Ricky Hill creating plenty of chances. It was a fantastic end-to-end game throughout. Georgie Berry scored the opening goal for us down at the Boothen End. Chambo had the ball right where the edge of the penalty area adjoins the goal line, but he was facing the corner flag with two defenders right up his backside, and yet somehow he managed an extraordinary twist to swivel on a sixpence and get a chipped cross into the near post. Because there didn't seem to be any danger, Luton's defenders had relaxed a bit, but George knew what Chambo was capable of and stayed switched on ready for the cross to come in, so he was able to steal a march on his defender and get to the ball first, dive headlong and nod the ball home. That was a fantastic goal.

To be honest Mark Chamberlain was unplayable at that time. He murdered just about every full-back he came up against for the first half of that season. The poor Luton defender up against him was Richard Money, who went on to play for Liverpool, so was no mug, but he had no answer to Chambo. It was incredible to think he'd been playing in the Fourth Division a month beforehand.

Georgie Berry was a good player too, vastly underrated, particularly for his character in the dressing room, but I always preferred him outside my box! He could be a bit of a danger inside his own penalty area! He did have the occasional mishap, including a couple of great headers he scored against me, but he was great to play with. He gave everything. I would have him in front of me every time.

PAUL WALSH EQUALISED when he lashed a stinging shot past me from distance before George scored with another header from a corner to put us 2-1 up – and that's when my trouble started.

·As I went up the tunnel feeling sorry for myself, of course the team were having to reorganise. They decided to put Paul Bracewell in goal in the immediate aftermath of my dismissal. He did OK, but just before the break Brian Stein scored to level things up at 2-2.

I just felt numb, although I did shed a few tears at half-time when the lads came in. I was feeling so guilty. But there was a lot going on in the dressing room, so I didn't get much of a chance to say sorry, or to get any sympathy either! The lads decided to change goalkeeper as they wanted Paul Bracewell out on the pitch to give them a better midfield shape, so Derek Parkin went in goal. As well as that, Mickey Thomas had cut his knee very badly. It was a huge gash and he had blood pouring off him. It couldn't be stitched and he ended up having to come off early in the second half, even though he'd tried desperately to carry on. I think that was one of the defining moments for him with the Stoke fans, as he became a real cult hero. So we had all that commotion going on and half-time went by in a flash.

It turned out to be a great decision as Bracewell scored the next goal. Just after half-time… a very rare Paul Bracewell goal. I mean that was what really made the game. We were down to ten men, with Mickey Thomas off and still we managed to take the lead again. It really was fantastic.

But with eleven men, Luton fought back and scored twice in ten minutes to take the lead 4-3. It was quite a warm day and they'd got in front and had a lot of experience and were very professional, so I thought that was it then, but football is such a wonderful game. It can be so unpredictable.

We kept striving to get forward and I remember this ball being hit to the edge of the Luton penalty area and it got headed down and fell at the feet of Brendan O'Callaghan, who hit it on the half volley on the run. He caught it perfectly and it fair flew into the back of the net. What a great goal and the players went absolutely wild. They were dancing and singing. That was with about five minutes to go, so now it was all hands to the pump to hang on for a point.

But just when you thought that all the twists and turns had gone, this game came up with one final stomach-churner in injury time.

Did Parkin bring the player down for a pen, and if so why was he not sent off a goalscoring opportunity?

And I'm thinking that's what the rule was brought in for. He brought him down and that became part of the referee's video as well.

But you just got the feeling this wasn't over yet. Obviously with a penalty taker as good as David Moss you just didn't expect him to miss. He was an absolutely fantastic penalty taker and here he was facing our full-back as the goalkeeper. Derek Parkin would not have had a clue about how Moss took his penalties and so wouldn't have been able to anticipate it, not like I did. I used to watch *Match of the Day* and the *Big Match* and any penalties I saw I used to note them down in a little notebook so I knew how players I might face took their penalties. We didn't have scouting reports as such like they have today. That's actually part of what I do now. I coach goalkeepers at Rochdale and Blackpool and then scout upcoming opponents for Rochdale, in particular looking at set pieces, penalty takers, dangermen and formations. Back then not every game had cameras at it, so you only had three or four a week to watch, so it wasn't as easy as it is now with Sky TV's coverage.

But that game had been so incredible, so full of incident and now Moss, with the chance to win it 5-4, was having to face the whole Boothen End, who were doing everything they could to put him off. I remember as David ran up I thought, 'I think there's going to be yet another twist here. Derek's going to save this.' And then David hit the ball and Derek didn't move, so I knew that wasn't going to happen! But then there was this great cheer as the ball smacked into the foot of the post and Dave Watson cleared it to safety. You could see all of Luton's energy sap out of them and the crowd were suddenly all up again cheering and shouting and screaming. It was absolutely amazing.

I really think that the Boothen End had helped massively in making Moss miss that penalty and keep the final score 4-4. The supporters who populated that end didn't realise what an effect they had. We'd have eight or ten thousand people on there for home games and they'd make an incredible noise. They could lift you and really make you feel special. Just to see them all cheering as you ran out was enough to inspire me. I always used to think, 'At least I've got all of them on my side today.'

Being a goalkeeper I spent a lot of time during my 400 or so games standing at that end of the ground just in front of the Boothen. I always got a great reception and it really did give me a lift and help me with my performance level.

In one of my very early games for Stoke, when I was deputising for the injured Roger Jones, I'd dropped a cross against Crystal Palace in front of the Boothen End and Brendan O'Callaghan sliced the ball into the net and we lost 2-1. Alan Durban was not impressed with me and told me in no uncertain terms that I would not play for the first team again. He tried to get someone in on loan for the midweek League Cup tie we were due to play against Third Division Swindon, but he couldn't manage it, so I played anyway. And I got a lot of positives from the crowd. They really helped me put the mistake behind me.

I got to know a lot of supporters as well. I loved to go out and meet them and I became one of them. I used to sign any autograph that was put in front of me because I always felt I was privileged to play for these people. I was only Peter Fox, son of a steel worker from Sheffield, after all. I was just doing what I did. I feel that's missing in the game today. That bond is missing and I know it helped me in those days when I had a few tough times.

CHAMBO WAS MAGNIFICENT that day, especially that spin for the cross for the first goal. The following week that was used by Jimmy Greaves on ITV's *Saint and Greavesie* to start his campaign to get Chambo into the England team. That came off when Mark was selected for his first cap shortly afterwards. I had also been talked about as being in terms of being in England contention. That was great as it came out quite early in the season that England were going to go on a post-season tour of Australia and Ray Clemence had said that he was not going to go. He wanted the summer off as there wasn't a major tournament, so that left a space in the squad and I was told that it would be between myself or Nigel Spink at Aston Villa as to who would be given the chance. Well, we were above Villa at the time and we continued to have a good season past Christmas and into March, so I thought I had a good chance. But with us in seventh position we sold Dave Watson and consequently had a disastrous run in and ended up 13th. It was a massive mistake to sell Dave Watson; a massive, massive mistake. He was the glue that held our defence together. He was a great talker and organiser and without him we nose-dived over those last few games, when a good run in would have seen us qualify for Europe. Who knows what would have happened then. Instead he was allowed to go over to the States and join Vancouver Whitecaps for a paltry fee.

During that period we got hammered 4-0 at Villa and I am sure they had a scout there to check out the pair of us. 4-0 was hardly going to show me up well and, of course, Nigel got the call. I think the sending off against Luton had an effect too as it never looked good on your copybook in those days if you had been dismissed. In fact often they wouldn't select you for England if you were serving a domestic suspension. Imagine that now!

I HAD TO really work to be able to perform as a top flight keeper. I was never the tallest goalkeeper in the world, but in my day the perfect height for a goalkeeper was 6ft. Nowadays, of course, it's more like 6ft 4in, but I didn't even make the requisite height back then. I was only ever 5ft 10½. Even if I stretched I couldn't quite make 5ft 11in! But I was only an inch and a quarter off what was considered the required height. I remember the first time I played against Peter Shilton, I shook hands with him at the end of the game and I was actually taller than him. He really wasn't that big. People just thought he was because of the aura he presented and because his ability made him seem so big. But don't believe him when he tells you he's 6ft. I was taller than him.

I did a lot of leg weights as I worked on getting more spring into my legs to compensate for my height. I used to put weights on my back and run up and down the Boothen End and then I would do the same at home too, up and down the stairs. I worked on my shot-stopping and my reactions as well. But I think also I was a very good reader of the game and the perfect match for me was if I didn't have a shot to save, as that meant I had influenced the players in front of me to keep the ball away from my goal.

When I first joined Stoke the coach was a guy named Wally Gould and he used to like staying behind after training and working with me, either taking shots or putting crosses in for me to practise dealing with. It was a bit of fun really, but we spent hours there working on that side of my game. Then I was lucky because Gordon Banks came in and coached me for two years. That was fantastic because he had dodgy hips and one eye and he could still catch the frigging ball cleaner than I could! He really used to annoy me at times!! He used to tell me how when he started at Chesterfield he would train on a Sunday, even after games on a Saturday, and you could understand how he made himself into a truly great goalkeeper and I aspired to be like him.

I GOT MY opportunity when Alan Durban decided to give me a chance to have a run in the first team from Boxing Day 1979. It was against Manchester City and we drew 1-1. Late in the game I made a good save from Michael Robinson from about 12 yards out. He hit a volley and I dived to my left and hung on to the ball. Actually I thought it was a decent save, but a reasonably comfortable one. But in the press it was all, 'what a fantastic save' and 'Fox saves a point', which is exactly what you want as a young keeper looking to make an impression.

I have played more games for Stoke City than any other goalkeeper and I am very, very proud of that fact. It's a record that probably won't be beaten. It's all the better because of the goalkeepers that Stoke have had; Gordon Banks, Peter Shilton, even John Farmer, who by all accounts was a top keeper. To follow in their footsteps was a pleasure and an honour. I remember when I went down to Exeter after I had finished at Stoke, a local press man came to interview me and he asked me how I felt about taking over the gloves from their club legend Kevin Miller, who'd just been sold to Birmingham. And I said, "Well, you know, I'll try and do my best. Of course when I went to Stoke they'd had Banks and Shilton and I played over 400 games there and they were quite happy with me." What a prat! Kevin Miller, who's he? Apparently a legend in south Devon!

MY LONGEVITY AT Stoke did, of course, present me with something of a problem as far as this book is concerned. I had so many games that I could have chosen. Beating Liverpool 2-0 in 1984 came close, as I remember the feeling driving home after that game. I was really flying. Even in Leek, where I lived, you could see people smiling and happy. Another good match for me was a televised 2-0 win over Tottenham in 1982 because it contained a commentary line that said something like, "That's another great save from Fox." Their side contained the likes of Hoddle, Archibald and Clemence and I've still got the tape, which I do watch occasionally.

We beat Manchester United a couple of times, which was always good, and there was the game in the fifth round of the cup in 1987 against eventual winners Coventry City, which they always say was the hardest game they had on their way to Wembley.

One match that sticks in my mind, but wasn't in contention at all, was when we went to play in a post-season tournament in Tampa Bay. It was right at the end of the old NASL and they used to have all this ridiculously elaborate, over-the-top stuff going on around the match. For example I had a monkey chained behind the goal and it would climb all the way along my crossbar and down the other side. Not off-putting at all!

And then their striker was sent through in a one-on-one with me and as he got to the edge of the box he shot. It beat me, hit the bar and came down on to the line. And as it's bounced down, all of a sudden there was this huge explosion. Bang!

All the lads hit the deck. They were all crapping themselves. We'd been shot at!

Of course no one had bothered to tell us that they used the cannon which was meant for the American Football team, who were nicknamed the Buccaneers, to celebrate goals for the soccer team. As the ball had hit the bar and bounced down, the bloke who operated the cannon thought it had gone in, so he's set it off and we've all flung ourselves down leaving the striker to head home the rebound. We lost 3-1!

America has a lot to answer for in terms of football. If you kicked the ball as far as the halfway line you got a standing ovation – and I was only punting the ball upfield like I did countless times every single game. The crowd just didn't appreciate the game at all, they'd be up and yelling and whooping just because you'd kicked the ball 50 yards, not because it was an accurate kick or under pressure or anything.

I remember Gordon Banks saying that he felt when he moved to play there all they were actually interested in was the fact he was only had full use of one eye. He was put on to a horse to enter the stadium for his debut amidst all this razzamatazz and he thought that all the fans had only turned up to see the best one-eyed goalkeeper in the world!

WHEN I JOINED the club in 1978 I was given the locker next to Denis Smith and when I left 15 years later I had seen so many other players use the other lockers it made me feel really old! I was even beginning to be called a veteran, which hurt; it really hurt! Because even then I didn't feel like a veteran.

But it gave me so many great games to chose from and only one choice allowed. It was tough to pluck the Luton match out of the hat. For example, winning the Autoglass Trophy was a special moment for me too.

We'd gone down under Mills and Ball. Mick had spent over £1m in the summer of 1989. That annoyed me – not because he bought a replacement keeper or anything; far from it, he didn't. No, it was because the week before that I had gone to see him to ask for a pay rise. He had fobbed me off by saying that he hadn't got any money. I asked for just a tenner more to show that after all these years the club valued me. But then, just a week or so later, he went out and bought a clutch of players for over a million quid! And those players didn't make the team any better. They didn't give us a spark and we really struggled that season.

I'll never really understand why Alan Ball didn't work out at Stoke because he brought so much passion to his work and that's what Stokies like to see. I liked his methods of getting you wound up before games, but a lot of the lads didn't. They thought it was too intense. But it got the best out of me. But for whatever reason he fell out with the fans and got driven out of town after relegation.

Lou Macari revitalised the club and brought in a lot of good signings for peanuts like Steino, Overson and Gleghorn. Vince was a great signing. He was a man's man on the pitch. Yes, he was arrogant, but that was all part of him. I mean, before the game if there was a mirror around you wouldn't be able to get in front of it because Vince would be there, sorting his hair out. And after the game he'd be using bubble bath, face scrubs and moisturiser and we used to think, "My god! Look at the state of him!" But if there was a cross coming into the area, he'd put his head on it, no mistake. I would love a Vince Overson in any team I was involved in.

But I nearly didn't play in the Autoglass final for several reasons. Firstly Lou told me I was too old. He brought in Jason Kearton on loan from Everton, but Lou couldn't get the deal sorted to sign him permanently because Everton didn't want him cup-tied, so I played in the cups that year. Even when Lou brought Ronnie Sinclair in permanently from Walsall later in the season, he'd already played in the Autoglass Trophy, ironically against Stoke, and so was cup-tied and I got back into the team, which left me to play at Wembley.

Don't let anyone tell you that it was 'only' the Autoglass Trophy. Any appearance at Wembley is to be cherished. Having got over the selection hurdle, I nearly didn't make it because of injury. On the

Monday morning during training we were doing our usual jogging around the Vic and I slipped on a piece of polythene sheeting and twisted my ankle. I couldn't train all week. The team went to a health farm following the disappointment of the play-off semi-final defeat on the Wednesday night. That was brilliant. It was a real good bonding session, which I needed because I'd been almost totally out of the first team picture that season. In fact I realised I wasn't really that important to Lou and his staff when, on the Friday before the final, I was still struggling with my ankle and instead of showing some sympathy towards me and helping me get better, the staff were all talking about who they could get in on emergency loan!

But to play at Wembley was great. I loved every minute of it. There was a tear in my eye driving to the ground. When you dream about going to Wembley you dream about the bus edging through crowds of your fans as you get near the ground and that's exactly what happened. I was there living the dream. It was wonderful. Very emotional, although I had to keep those emotions in check.

We didn't start particularly well and Stockport had the ball in the net early on, but the referee pulled them up for a foul on me. The thing was that I didn't actually think it was a foul at all, but I got away with that one. We gradually took control and went 1-0 up on a very hot day and we did most of the attacking after that.

My abiding memory is of the 40,000 or so Stoke fans singing all our names after the final whistle and I really understood after that why they say that if you are going to go to Wembley, make sure you win. The Stockport players looked utterly gutted.

It's a long walk up those steps and I was second up there, so I took the cup from Vince Overson when he handed it on back through the team. We did a lap of honour and I remember seeing the guy who is now the assistant manager of Crewe, Neil Baker. He was manager of Leek Town at the time and there he was on top of the perimeter fencing at Wembley screaming at the top of his voice, "We are Stoke!" I couldn't believe it – I said, "Eh up, Bake! How are you?" I can still remember him now, this grown man going crazy. It was a magnificent day.

I THINK THE other game in contention was the match which clinched the Second Division title in April 1993. I played the last ten games of that season after on loan Bruce Grobbelaar had been recalled by Liverpool and it was past transfer deadline day so Macari had to play me. I only conceded five goals in ten games and the team were playing well, but a lot of nerves were starting to kick in. I had been on loan at Linfield for a few months and came back bouncing and full of beans. I think a few of the lads were twitchy because of what had happened the previous season where the team had caved in after leading the table in mid-April. And we'd now got this last game at home against Plymouth in which we needed the three points to confirm both promotion and the Championship. Nigel Gleghorn scored very early on to put us 1-0 up, and you would have thought that would have settled the nerves, but actually it only served to add to them as we now had the finishing line in our sights.

Then I made a double save from Warren Joyce. I stopped his first shot from inside the area and then got up quickly to smother his follow-up. If I say so myself I think that was a world class save. I still see Warren Joyce now and remind him about that save. But I remember I made another fingertip save right at the death as well.

We all went out into Newcastle and had a fantastic night. And I was delighted that I could help the club win promotion and I could win a medal. It was a great way to round off my Stoke career.

BRENDAN O'CALLAGHAN: BORN 23 JULY 1955, BRADFORD; 294 GAMES, 47 GOALS

Brendan O'Callaghan

Stoke City 1 Manchester United 0

League Division One

Wednesday 2 March 1983

I'D BEEN PLAYING professional football for ten years, first at Doncaster and then at Stoke and I had never beaten Manchester United. I was desperate to beat them. Desperate.

I'd scored a couple of goals against them, and we'd drawn the odd match, but I had never beaten them and that really irked me.

Ron Atkinson's United were the best team in the country at that time as they had not been beaten in the whole of 1983, and we were now in March. To put it in some perspective, United won the FA Cup that season, finished third in the league after having had a horrible run before Christmas, and lost the League Cup final to Liverpool, so at the very least they were the best team that calendar year, if not the entire season as Liverpool won the league.

Added to that was the fact that their centre-half was Gordon McQueen, who I'd played against on my debut,, and I'd had so many battles with him over the years, from his time at Leeds and then at Old Trafford, that he was almost a friend! The other centre-half was a young Paul McGrath, who went on to become a great player, so I was pleased that I got the better of them

The clinching reason for me that I chose this game was because I feel that I played my best match for Stoke that night. Certainly it was my best game as a centre-forward against one of the best teams around.

I'D MADE SOMETHING of a whirlwind start to my Stoke career when I signed for Alan Durban in March 1978 from Doncaster

Rovers. He was the new manager after the sacking of George Eastham. After warming the bench for what should have been my first game at Crystal Palace on the Saturday, I found myself there again as we played Hull at home the following Tuesday. The team were struggling for the breakthrough and as I warmed up along the touchline towards the Boothen End the crowd started chanting my name. They hadn't had a big centre-forward since John Ritchie and they'd missed someone like that. When we won a corner kick they called my name again and so Durban decided to put me on. I was that keen to get on and make my debut

The last thing he said to me as I waited to enter the pitch was, "Are you going to get me a goal." So I said, "Yes." Of course I did. What else are you going to say? But now the myth is that I predicted I'd score. Then I jogged into the penalty area and the corner came over and I got up at the near post to flick a header into the net – at the Boothen End as well! That was incredible.

I got into the team then and we had a good run in to the end of season, moving ourselves from 15th when I joined to a final seventh place. Of course the following season we won promotion thanks to that last day win at Notts County. I'm sure plenty of people would have thought I would select that match as my favourite game, but I actually didn't think that promotion side fulfilled its potential. For example Garth Crooks had fallen out with the manager and also coach Howard Kendall and he didn't play that well that season. He only really scored penalties and it was a shame because I thought we could have really hit it off, but Durban signed Paul Randall from Bristol Rovers to take Crooks' place and played Garth wide on the left. Even in that Notts County game Crooks on the wing and Randall and myself were up front. Crooks didn't like that, but the first year in the top league Garth got his act together and had a really good season. His contract was running out and I thought he was playing to get away. Indeed Spurs signed him in the summer of 1980.

Durban got criticised for playing boring football when we first went up, but he was just making sure we didn't go straight back down. I remember after a goalless draw at Highbury someone asked him why his teams weren't any more entertaining and he replied,

"If you want entertainment, send in the clowns." I think he was set up to say that to be honest, but he was quite happy keeping us afloat and then bringing in better quality over the summer with the money he got for Garth Crooks' sale.

He brought in some good players and gradually built a side, but he'd got frustrated by a lack of ambition and he in the following summer he was offered the earth to go and turn Sunderland around. The first thing I knew about it was on our post-season tour to the Caribbean, although I'd heard a rumour that he might be going back to his old club Derby. Before we flew out to the West Indies, I remember Percy Axon, the chairman, asked me to have a word with Durban while we were out there to persuade him to stay. Well to be honest I loved Percy, but it wasn't my job to do that. It was his. It was a bit presumptuous of him to ask me. As a player, you can't go telling managers that they should stay with you.

I learnt later that the board had allowed Durban's contract to run out, so he was in a strong position because he was quite within his rights to talk to whoever he wanted. He chose Sunderland because of what was on offer, which I think was a blunder on his part, but it was a major error by Stoke because Durban had brought through all these good youngsters like Heath, Bracewell, Chapman and Ursem. Had he stayed, they probably would have stayed too. Durban had created such a good atmosphere at the club, but it all got ruined.

In fact I still feel that the best Stoke side I played with was in the second half of the 1980/81 season when under Durban we pulled ourselves into a solid mid-table position after only just surviving in our first season following promotion.

I ALWAYS THOUGHT if Durban's replacement Richie Barker had kept those youngsters we'd have had a really good team for the future. As it was he went with older, short-term acquisitions like Sammy McIlroy, Mickey Thomas, Robbie James and Paul Dyson. Barker had this wonderful ability to fall out with players! When he eventually left I think there were seven players on the transfer list at their own request, including me and I was the captain at the time!

Despite that, in the summer of 1982 Richie did bring in some good players like Mickey Thomas and Mark Chamberlain. It was funny actually because I always felt that Barker stumbled on to that 82/83 team. I know, for example, that Chambo and Mickey Thomas weren't top of Barker's shopping list, which was why they weren't brought in until just before the season started. I'm not sure he was really after, but luckily for us it all just clicked together. And a good job too as we'd had a pretty inauspicious pre-season that year, losing to Wokingham and Linfield and on tour to Viking Stavanger. We hadn't played very well and it was clear that the squad, without most of those younger players wasn't going to be good enough.

I started the season playing up front alongside Paul Maguire. He wasn't really a striker, more of a player like Wayne Rooney who could play in the hole behind the front two and be creative, or out wide. Halfway through the season Barker gave Ian Painter his chance alongside me and we were much more of a threatening pairing. Ian was small and pacy and very fit. He had a good eye for goal as well and scored in vital wins over Ipswich, Brighton and Watford. We worked well together and Ian made the position his own.

We were very solid at the back. Peter Fox was the best goalkeeper I ever played with. People always hold his lack of height against him, but I never ever saw him get dominated in the air. He was the best shot-stopper I think I saw in the game and I always felt he was a great ice hockey netminder because he was always impossible to beat in the gym. Had he been those couple of inches taller he would have undoubtedly gone on to play for England.

Foxy was a great character and Paul Maguire and I got on really well with him. Foxy was sponsored by Saab and he had to go and do these various events and appearances to fulfil his obligations to get his sponsored car. So he asked myself and Paul and Peter Hampton if we wanted to join him on this sponsor's day at Silverstone race track. So we travelled down in Foxy's car. Now the reason we wanted to go was because we could sign up to drive a Saab turbo around the track, but when we got there at around half past nine, we couldn't get a slot until 3pm. So while Foxy had to go and press the flesh along with other celebrities like Des Lynam, Ian Botham and

Angela Rippon. Peter, Paul and I said we'd drive into the local town and find a pub, because, of course, being a race track, Silverstone was dry.

Foxy had a Saab 99, which was at the lower end of the range, and he gave Paul Maguire the keys so he could drive us into the town. Two or three hours later, when we had a couple or three and we were in fine form, Paul drove us back to the track. As we approached the pits, we got waved into this garage and instead of stopping he just drove through it and on to the track! The car was totally unprepared for going round there. We were doing about 80mph, but these other cars were doing 120mph easy. Paul had no idea about driving on the track and he was taking the hairpins up on two wheels rather than cutting across them using the racing line. There was no getting away from the fact it was us because on the side of the car it said in big letters 'Stoke City's No. 1 and Sweden's No. 1 team up at Hinton's of Leek,' so it was definitely Foxy's car! Paul drove round the complete track laughing his high-pitched infectious laugh which started us off. We were absolutely in tears laughing. Once we pulled up, Foxy came over because his dad had told him that he'd seen his car going round the track and his mouth was hanging open and he just said, "I don't believe it."

The club had characters everywhere you looked. We used to have a father and son pair who were groundsmen at the Victoria Ground; Derek and Eddie, the Hartleys. And they used to shoot the pigeons out of the roofs of the stands. Eddie in particular hated people going on the pitch. He was meticulous in his preparation of it. He used to cut it in circles, emanating out from the centre spot. Foxy used to take no notice of this and he would go out there and practise in the middle of the pitch, rolling all over the place, ruining all Eddie's patterns. I remember this one day, Eddie got so fed up with Foxy that he pulled the shotgun out and fired it above his head. Foxy's face was a picture! Eddie had lost it. He was shouting, "I told you not to go on there!"

Of course one of the biggest characters was Georgie Berry. I always felt George would have been a better success story if he'd been given man-marking duties and he certainly always played better when he had a talker alongside him. Ironically, class payer though he was, his partner that season Dave Watson was not a great talker on the pitch. He led by example. I think George had his best days at Wolves when he had Emlyn Hughes alongside him, who never stopped talking! Sometimes George struggled with zonal marking responsibility as he was really looking to mark a player, not the space, but you always knew you would get 100 per cent effort from him.

I HAD ACTUALLY played at the back alongside Dave Watson on occasions the previous season because of necessity and had learnt a lot from him about positional play. I always felt comfortable at the back, although I preferred playing up front, but needs must. I just switched my thinking around, so I thought about what I would not like as a centre-forward and did just that as a defender. I didn't mind getting switched around as I didn't get stale, there was always a fresh challenge.

I also played alongside Mike Doyle, who was another player from Manchester who came down to finish his career and have a swansong at Stoke in the top flight after being rejected by so-called bigger club. The main thing I learnt from Mike was about arrogance on the field. He genuinely thought he was a better player than anyone else on the pitch and he would put that across to the other players. If he sensed the slightest bit of weakness in the opposition he would pounce upon it. I remember when we played Aston Villa the year they won the Championship (1980/81) and Mike picked on their little forward, Gary Shaw, who played alongside Peter Withe up front. I was marking Withe and Doyle was marking Shaw and we did really well against them. Shaw had a perma-tan and was clearly a bit of a pretty boy and fancied himself a bit. I remember Doyle constantly having a go at him, you know, "Did the sun lamp burst?", "Have you shaved your legs today?", "Bad time of the month?" That sort of thing. He was at him all game.

I also remember that Mike was hated by Manchester United fans because of what he'd got up to when playing for City against them. They were always having a go at him Apparently there had been one or two inflammatory incidents with George Best and Lou Macari. In fact I believe Doyle holds the record for the most sendings off in Manchester derbies. This time we were playing at Old Trafford and we managed a 2-2 draw and someone in the Stretford End threw a watch at him and Doyle picked it up and put it in his pocket!.

People often say that Alan Hudson was arrogant, but I don't agree. Huddy was never truly arrogant. He had a strut and a confidence, but it was only construed as arrogance. He wasn't actually an arrogant person. He just was so much better a footballer than everyone else around and he proved that in both spells he had at Stoke.

Of course our midfield from that season is legendary now and when you've got a midfield quartet like that you are going to play football, but there are times when you need an outlet ball up front and I acted as the target man when I played up front and that allowed Mickey Thomas to come roaming in from the left looking for the knockdowns. It was my job to get hold of the ball, allow the midfield players to get in touch and bring them into play. It could be scintillating at times.

WE HAD BEEN playing really well that season and we really did fancy our chances in this game. To be honest I think that the Britannia Stadium is fantastic as a modern ground, but it is also fantastic for the visiting teams as well. I mean, whoever designed it got it totally wrong when they put the tunnel next to the away fans. That's just stupid. But you also don't get the intimidating atmosphere that you did at the Vic. It's too open. The old ground felt so much more homely to us and intimidating to the visitors. When we came out of the tunnel both sides of it were lined with Stoke fans shouting abuse at the visiting team and it felt as if the fans were almost on the pitch at times, so they could let the opposition know what they thought. Add into all that the state of the pitch, which was almost always muddy, apart from the first few games of the season, and you'd got quite an advantageous situation. The problem with the Brit is it's very sanitised. It's modern things like Health and Safety, I suppose, and complying with the Taylor Report into all-seater stadia, but you can't help thinking all that helps the away side more than Stoke.

That night against United the Boothen was in full cry and it really helped us keep going and pressing home our advantage. Mark Chamberlain was magnificent, giving his full-back Arthur Albiston a right roasting. Mark was great for me because, despite the fact I was a big centre-forward, I had never really played with a winger at Stoke. In fact Terry Conroy had been the last winger I'd had. Chambo could beat any full-back in the country, he was that good.

I understand Mark's chosen the game against Birmingham earlier that season as his match. He was incredible there, running them ragged and scoring those two great goals. I would just like to take a moment to claim the assist on Chambo's first goal, because I passed to him on the halfway line, setting him up for that 50-yard tap in!

We'd been playing so well as a team that for once we felt that we could take United on. We had lost 1-0 up at Old Trafford early in the season to a very late Bryan Robson goal when they had been top of the table and we felt we'd deserved something out of the game, but we'd missed two or three good chances. I remember that match was on *Match of the Day* and when I saw it that night I couldn't believe how well we'd played and yet we'd still come away with nothing. I was determined to make up for that and I can honestly say that I had the feeling we were going to finally beat them.

They had some magnificent players. Frank Stapleton, who was a great centre-forward and was always going to give any central defender a hard time. Alongside him they had Norman Whiteside, who had hit the headlines with his performances as a 17-year-old at the 1982 World Cup in Spain. On the right wing they had Steve Coppell, who was probably Mark Chamberlain's only serious contender for the title of Best Right-Winger in Britain. Then there were those two international central defenders, so they had a top team out.

I actually should have had a hat-trick against United, but Gary Bailey was in goal and he pulled off two tremendous world class saves from two of my headers from Chamberlain crosses from 12 yards out, scooping them off the line to keep the scoresheet blank. I think those first two headers were actually better ones than the one that did find the net. I'd got more power in them. But then a cross came in from the left from Mickey Thomas and I flung myself at it and headed towards goal, albeit not as well as those first two. Perhaps that's what helped that header beat him. I had really powered those first two headers and this one I didn't connect with as powerfully, I kind of glanced it in and it beat Bailey to find the back of the net.

United didn't really make a clear-cut chance. Dave Watson and George Berry at the heart of our defence totally bossed Stapleton and Whiteside. They really hadn't had a kick.

1-0, I think, flattered them on the night and I think it shows we were competing at the very highest level, and that the result wasn't a fluke either. I remember after the game Sammy McIlroy made a comment that he was disappointed with young Whiteside because essentially Sammy had been released in favour of him and he felt he was still a better player. Mickey Thomas had also been released by Ron Atkinson soon after he'd arrived at United, so he enjoyed it considerably too. But I don't think it was a case of United not fancying it at all. I think that would be very harsh on us because we played so well, taking the game to them and taking them on head to head.

We had a couple of pints at the club and then went up to a pub called the Ash Bank and there was a lot of singing and celebrating going on because we felt we had beaten the biggest club in the world on their own terms and we now felt we were competing on the same stage as a club as big as Manchester United.

In fact that meant we had the Indian sign over United then! We must have done because they were one of only three teams we beat in that horrible relegation season. That was a great win, but much more of a fluke than the victory I have chosen. This match we felt we had the all-round strength to take them on, utilising our strong midfield.

One other thing that sticks in my mind from after that win was that I spoke to both Alan Durban, my former manager, and Alan Dodd, who had just moved to Wolves after ten years at Stoke, and both said that they hadn't seen me play as well before. So that really clinched it for me. It was confirmation that this was indeed the match of my life.

IAN PAINTER: BORN 28 DECEMBER 1964, WOMBORNE; 123 GAMES, 24 GOALS

Ian Painter

Stoke City 2 Liverpool 0

League Division One

Saturday 14 April 1984

I'LL HAVE TO own up and tell you that I'm a West Brom fan. I grew up in the Black Country and still live there today. I suppose I should by rights have signed for West Brom, or even Walsall, where I also trained as a kid, but it was circumstance that brought me to Stoke.

I was always mad keen on football and played for a crack team called Prestwood Colts. Mark Walters (who went on to star for Aston Villa and Liverpool), Steve Davis (Burnley), Ian Cartwright (Wolves) and goalkeeper Phil Pritchard (Stoke City) also played for them. We were a good side and attracted a lot of attention. We used to play the cup finals we got to at the West Brom training ground and that's where the five of us who played pro football all got spotted

At the time the chief scout of Sheffield United was a guy called Neville Briggs. He spotted me and had made contact with my dad and it seemed as if I was going to sign for the Blades, but in mid-1978 Neville got the job as chief scout at Stoke and he took all of the lads that he'd been nurturing with him for Sheffield United to train at Stoke. I really enjoyed it up there, much more than I ever had at West Brom or Walsall, where I'd also trained, and because I had such a good laugh I stayed at Stoke and began to make progress. It was such a warm friendly club.

Then one day, when I was 15, after I'd been playing for the youth team for a while, the coach Tony Lacey asked me to go and make up the numbers in the reserve team that was playing an eleven-a-side match against the first team. All of a sudden I was playing against Denis Smith and Mike Pejic and that really made my mind up that this was a good club to be at because things were happening for me and I was getting involved, whereas at West Brom I hadn't kicked a ball in anger.

At 16, Stoke offered me an apprenticeship and I went into digs with Steve Lennon and Colin Singer, who were both 17 and got very friendly with some of the local lads like Steve Bould, and also Steve Parkin. We began to break into the first team around the same time. They were good times, because they were very level-headed lads and we had a lot of fun.

At first I was a right-winger, but when I got into the first team I couldn't play on the right because we'd got Mark Chamberlain there, so Richie Barker put me up front with Brendan O'Callaghan and it just clicked. I'd actually only played seven reserve games at that stage. One of the reasons I was successful was I was so fit. I had a great engine and that enabled me to chase people down from up front to give the back four a breather. They really appreciated the work I put in to unsettle opposing defences when they had the ball.

I DID SO well I got into the England Youth team and then the England under-21s, coached by former Manchester United manager Dave Sexton. The players I played with there like Paul Rideout and Tony Cottee were in the reserves at Swindon and West Ham respectively, but they were on a lot more money compared to me – and I was in Stoke's first team. I remember for get-togethers at Lilleshall I had to catch a train from Stoke down to Stafford and then get a taxi. Whereas Cottee turned up in his brand spanking new Ford XR3i!

Graham Taylor was the England Youth manager at the time. Graham was very much a long ball merchant and looked for people like me to get on to the second ball from a knockdown. He liked me because I could run all day. When I think I was in the side ahead of Cottee then and Graham went on to manage the full England side, I wonder if he'd have stuck with me if I'd stayed fit and been successful at Coventry and given me a chance. Given that players like Carlton Palmer got plenty of caps I'd like to think I'd have had a go. But you could see the way England were going then, and it was all long ball theory.

I remember a funny story about Carlton actually. He lived near me and we were both youngsters that had just broken into our first teams at Stoke and West Brom respectively, but he didn't recognise me, although I knew him. This one night we were in a local nightclub and I saw Carlton playing on the Space Invaders machine. He was totally concentrated on it, so I thought I'd have a bit of fun. I snuck over and turned the machine off and waited for him to look up and have a go at me, but he didn't. He kept on playing! And he went on and played for England?!

SO AS A 17-year-old at Christmas 1982 I broke into the Stoke first team and scored goals. I may only have been small, but actually my first three goals were all headers. I always felt my positioning and anticipation would get me into goalscoring positions.

My good form made me in demand. At one point I was very close to signing for Ipswich when they had a very good side down there. My brother got married and his new father-in-law happened to be the managing director of Ipswich and he phoned me up and said that their manager, Bobby Ferguson, wanted to sign me. I'd never thought about leaving up to that point, but soon after Ipswich came in, so did Manchester City.

Our coach Bill Asprey pulled me to one side in the gym one day and said he wanted a word. As I followed him out of the door, Dave Watson, who'd seen what was happening, pulled me to one side and said, "Before you sign for anyone, you come and see me." He knew exactly what was going on, and he'd been so successful in his career, playing for England and winning trophies with Man City, that I respected what he had to say. So I heard all about the offers from Bill, and what Stoke were prepared to offer me to stay, which was to treble what I was on to £350 a week.

The next day Dave Watson, who was generally a very quiet man, asked me what I'd negotiated, and I told him, and he asked me if I was happy, and I said, "yes." And he advised me to stay and carry on. So I did.

We had some tremendous old pros like Dave at Stoke and they all helped me in some way or other to become a better player and a better person. Our left-back Derek Parkin used to live in the Black Country as well and I'd got into the team so young I hadn't actually got my driving licence, so Derek used to give me a lift and I learnt so much from him. I loved listening to him talking about his time with Wolves and how he had managed to make a career as a left-back despite the fact he was right-footed. He used to practise his left foot so much.

Mickey Thomas was a legend. He was an unbelievable guy. Totally hyperactive. I can't possibly repeat half the things he said and did. He was hilarious though. It was as though his brain was switched into overdrive constantly. He could be easily led into trouble, though. Especially when he went out on the town in Rhyl. He had a great left foot and was a real scamp on the field.

JUST BEFORE THE start of the 1983/84 season we got the shock of our lives. We were training up at Keele University and Richie Barker had been on an FA training course at Lilleshall. He turned up with his clipboard and sat us all down and started telling us all these new ideas about Position Of Maximum Opportunity and the theory put about by FA Head Coach Charles Hughes that all goals come from moves of five passes or less and it soon became apparent that he basically just wanted to play long ball football. Well everyone looked at each other, and I listened to the likes of Sammy McIlroy and Mickey Thomas saying how they'd worked so bloody hard to become footballers that they weren't going to stand for playing like that. They started taking the mickey in training then, every time Barker stopped it and told them to play it long. I mean, when you think of the midfield we had! Chambo, Mickey Thomas, Sammy Mac and Paul Bracewell, it was basically the best in the top flight, and Barker decided to completely miss it out. It was crazy.

Anyway we went on a pre-season tour of Scandinavia and we started banging in all these goals. Well, no disrespect to some of the sides we played out there, but they weren't proper teams. We may have scored 23 goals in three games, but we knew we were in trouble when it came to the league starting up again. We hated playing that way and it didn't work. We lost five of the first six games and only scored in one of those games. By Christmas we were dead bottom of the league along with Wolves and Barker had been sacked. It was disastrous and a lot of the players who had made the 1982/83 season such a success had left.

But of course it all changed round when Alan Hudson came in. Bill Asprey had consulted all the more experienced players and said openly in a team meeting that he wanted to try and get out of the mire by reverting to playing football. I thought it was a bit strange as Bill had been the coach who had been implementing the long ball tactics under Barker. I found it difficult to get my head round that one.

So Huddy came in and it just clicked. Forget his drinking habits - we all drank, it was the way it was then - Alan Hudson trained harder than any pro I ever saw. He'd train in the mornings with us and then nick off afterwards and go and train in the local gym in the afternoons. But he didn't want the lads to know how much he was putting into it. He wanted to maintain his cool exterior, I suppose. I remember catching him one day when I was feeling a bit stiff after training and I went for a sauna - and there was Huddy doing sit-ups and trunk curls. That was amazing.

Huddy was a top bloke, a real character. We both love boxing and we'd always used to go to the Boxing Awards in London every October and then go on to the Conservative Club down the Embankment and just sit and chat about football. It was fantastic to talk to him. He always maintained that in the 1970s that England were totally wrong to leave out players such as Osgood, Currie and himself. Instead they picked workmanlike players. It was another period like the Taylor years.

I didn't know how good Huddy was until his first game against Arsenal. At half-time he pulled me to one side in the changing room and said, "Look, if you want the ball shout and point to where you want it and I'll put it there for you." So in the second half we began to strike up this partnership. I could play off him knowing that the ball would be delivered into the space I wanted to run into.

He also taught me how to control a ball and turn in one motion to beat a defender. Huddy could play the ball into me so that I would be able to turn on the side that the defender wasn't standing. He was phenomenal. He may have been a social animal when he was relaxing, but he was fantastic with me and his attitude to the game when he was switched on was superb.

That Arsenal game was won by a penalty scored by Paul Maguire, who was the dead ball specialist at the club, but after Paul left I took over the penalty taking duties. There wasn't any plan about that; I earned the first penalty myself. It was at home against Watford and I got brought down for the foul and actually landed on the ball. So it was stuck under my body and as I got up I picked it up. Sammy McIlroy had been taking them, so I threw it to him and he threw it me back and said, "I don't fancy it today. Do you fancy it?"

Of course I said, "Yes."

And he said, "You cocky sod"!

But I put the ball down and scored it and as I ran back to the halfway line I jogged past Sammy and said, "You won't get the ball back now, mate."

My technique was simply to hit the ball with pace towards the roof of the net. I used to practise and practise taking pens. It was quite a responsibility. I actually only missed the one penalty at Stoke. Thankfully hardly anyone was in the ground to see it as it was the final game of the horrible 1984/85 season against Coventry. We were 1-0 down and got this late penalty. If I scored it Coventry would be down as well as us, but I hit it over the top. That spared them and they stayed in the top flight for another 15 years or so.

WE SOMEHOW MANAGED to get ourselves back in with a chance of staying up in 1983/84 by playing some great football and winning a good run of games. But there was one fixture for me that stands out in that run because it was against simply the best team around at the time. That season Liverpool won the league and the League Cup, and also the European Cup final in Rome. They were a totally dominant team. For me it all started at the back where they had the superb defensive partnership of Alan Hansen and Mark Lawrenson. They were an amazing combination. I remember in one game at Liverpool I was sent clear and rounded Grobbelaar at the Kop end and stuck it in. But I was given offside and I was the only one in the ground that hadn't heard the whistle. I looked round and Hansen and Lawrenson were both there with their arms raised for offside stifling yawns!

Then up front Rush and Dalglish took some beating. Dalglish was a very special player. He was my idol and I wore No. 7 at Stoke because of him. It's a big thing wearing that shirt at Stoke, of course, because of Sir Stan. Liverpool won the game in which I 'scored' at Anfield 1-0 and as we trudged off the pitch, the two No. 7s together, I said, "Well played, Kenny."

And he replied, "Well done, Ian."

He knew my name! I was so pleased with that. I then spent the next week telling all my mates that Kenny Dalglish knew my name!

THIS LIVERPOOL GAME I have chosen was at Easter, so there was a big crowd because of the recovery we'd made and the fact it was a holiday. I'll always remember the controversy that went with it for me. No one knows about this, but despite the fact we played brilliantly and won the game, myself and a lad called Colin Russell, who was on loan from Huddersfield, had an argument over who scored the first goal. Colin was from Merseyside and a Liverpool fan, and he'd actually begun his career at Liverpool before moving on to a few lower league clubs like Bournemouth and Huddersfield. Colin wasn't much taller than me, so we had this tiny strike force, but we were both nippy and buzzed around the Liverpool defence.

I remember Chambo had a blinder on the wing. He tore into Phil Neal, the full-back. Halfway though the first half Chambo beat Neal yet again and hit a cross shot from just inside the box which Grobbelaar parried. I went in on it at the same time as Colin Russell, but I got to the ball and finished it by nicking it over Grobbelaar to make it 1-0 to Stoke. Colin had lunged to get there as well, but I had definitely got there first and knocked it in. Anyway, I turned round to celebrate only to see Russell running off claiming my goal. There was no way he had touched the ball at all! But apparently from one side of the ground it looked like he'd got their first.

Anyway at half-time with us 1-0 ahead, I had to tackle him, so I said, "You know I scored it."

And he said, bold as brass, "No. I got it."

"You fucking didn't!"

And Sammy McIlroy tried to calm things down by saying, "Hey. It doesn't matter lads. We scored a goal didn't we?"

And I said, "No Sammy you're right. It doesn't matter…But I scored it!"

Colin being a Liverpool lad really wanted the goal. He'd probably got a load of mates there. For him to score against Liverpool must have meant everything, especially as the club had rejected him. But his moment was to come. That goal was mine.

Then Colin was at it again in the second half. We got a free kick out on the left and Sammy McIlroy, who was a real quality player, took it and bent it around the two-man wall towards the far post. It came across at about waist height and Colin bent down and flung himself at it. Well to this day I don't know if he actually got a touch, but at the very least, him going for the ball made Grobbelaar stay on his line and he was totally flat-footed as the ball continued on and went just inside the far post. I have no idea if Colin got a slight touch on the ball, but needless to say he was off celebrating as if he had! Let's be charitable and say he scored that one – he's certainly in the record books as having scored it. But I can't remember if Sammy Mac thought that one didn't matter!

In fact, at the end of the game, one reporter came up to me and told me that Colin was still claiming both goals!

We played so well that game. We didn't allow them to create a real chance, because we had the ball most of the time. Liverpool had this way of playing away where they kept things tight and looked to score goals in the last 15 minutes, but they just couldn't get going. The supply to Rush was cut off and Dalglish was dropping deeper and deeper to try and find the ball.

THERE WAS A sideshow during the match. The entire game Souness was trying to cripple Huddy, but he couldn't get near him. I remember this one throw-in that came to Huddy and Souness was steaming into his back ready to take him down as he controlled it, but Souness ended up tackling thin air because Huddy had feinted to trap the ball and then let it run and skipped over the challenge. Souness was going redder and redder as the game went on as Huddy ran the entire show.

Then came an incident, which I think has gone down in Stoke folklore.

The previous season we'd played Anfield in the FA Cup and Richie had decided we'd play 5-4-1 with me up front. We went 1-0 down early on and Sammy McIlroy was looking over at Barker to see how we should change things, but he just kept it at five at the back. We were losing, but still defending. We couldn't understand it.

Graeme Souness was getting narked by the whole thing as we refused to make a game of it and at one point, he picked up the ball on the halfway line and found himself with 25 yards of space to run into because our team was all lined up halfway inside our own half. He had got so bored of this by now that he actually stopped the ball, sat on it and beckoned us forwards to try and tackle him. The funny thing was that not one of the team moved! Barker's tactics had been so drummed into us that the lads all stayed in position.

We'd taken some fearful hidings off Liverpool around then There were a couple of 5-1 defeats, including one at the Vic and so Barker had decided to close the game up and he was, I think, actually happy with a 2-0 defeat after Rush scored in the dying seconds.

But now with Bill Asprey in charge, Huddy in the side and some great football being played here we were 2-0 ahead and with a couple of minutes to go. One of the most professional players at the club was Brendan O'Callaghan, but he also had a bit of a twinkle in his eye and a good sense of humour. Big Bren was playing in defence that day and he picked the ball up from Foxy on the edge of the penalty area. All the Liverpool players had retreated to the halfway line expecting Peter to kick the ball upfield, so there was quite a distance between them and the ball. So Bren just put his foot on the ball a couple of yards outside the area, picked out Souness and beckoned him towards the ball. Souness went livid. He charged forwards and as he got near, Bren just neatly backheeled the ball into Foxy's waiting arms.

We all thought that was hilarious. Souness didn't. He was like an enraged bull. We hadn't talked about it or anything. Bren just did it. We were all thinking, "don't go upsetting these!"

Souness had a right strop on him – mind you Dalglish was particularly moody too that day – but Souness stormed off the pitch, pushed a copper out of the way, and put his hand through a glass and wiremesh window in the tunnel. He then turned round, with blood streaming off him, and screamed at Sammy Lee, "That should teach us a few fucking lessons."

He had this incredible desire to win. It was insatiable. I thought, "That is what winning means. That's what being a Liverpool player means."

AT THE TIME Stoke were on a par with the likes of Liverpool, Arsenal and Manchester United. We defeated them all at home in those three seasons. In fact I remember the day we beat United in the horrendous 1984/85 season, which in the context of that season was a superb result. It was Boxing Day and I'll never forget that particular game for a very personal reason. That morning Wolves had played Shrewsbury and a coach load of about 30 of my mates from the Black Country had been to see them. After their game had finished they all decided that they'd come up to watch me at Stoke. The first thing I knew about it was when the gaffer came into the changing room about an hour before kick-off and said to me, "There's a bloke at reception for you." So I went outside and there was my mate, who asked if he could have some tickets for the game, so I said, "sure, how many?"

"Thirty."

"Thirty?! Do you know who we're playing today – Man United!"

I went and saw the gaffer and he managed to sort out some tickets for me – I don't know where he got them from, but his attitude was, "the more the merrier." They had to pay for them, obviously, and they stood in the Boothen Stand paddock right behind the United dugout where manager Ron Atkinson stood. Of course, Big Ron was a former Albion man, so these Wolves supporters gave him fearful stick all game. And when I slammed a penalty past Gary Bailey into the roof of the net to equalise Frank Stapleton's opening goal, they got so excited, jumping up and down, that the dugout roof collapsed!

I remember when I scored the goal I first turned to the Boothen End, as I always did, but then I ran all the way round past the corner flag and along the Boothen Paddock until I found my mates along there. That was a great moment.

OBVIOUSLY THAT SEASON was a write-off because all we had was kids in the team. People like Phillip Heath, Carl Saunders and Chris Maskery, who were just too green to all be in the team together and we were down before the season had begun really. It was the beginning of the end for me at Stoke. I had this injury. My leg was killing me and no one could find out what it was. I had three epidurals to see if I could play, but I was turning into an old man very quickly. This one day I went with Alan Hudson to the races and he said to me that he'd spoken to someone at Coventry who was after me. Now Stoke had just been relegated and so it would mean a return to the First Division. But not only that, it would mean playing alongside my hero as a boy, Cyrille Regis, who'd made his name at West Brom and had become a god at Coventry. So Huddy put me in touch with the guy he was talking about and it turned out to be John Sillett, who was one half of the managerial partnership at Coventry at the time with George Curtis. John offered me double the money that I was on at Stoke and I began to realise I'd been stuck in a timewarp at the Victoria Ground as the club had fallen apart.

But I joined Coventry carrying this injury and it got so I really couldn't play. And when I told the gaffer this I got dropped out of the team and was blanked. I wasn't any use to them any more and they told me that I had to get it sorted out myself. Just my luck, that year Coventry won through to the FA Cup final, but I couldn't play. In fact my replacement that day was Keith Houchen, who, of course, scored that diving header to write himself a piece of Wembley history. He wouldn't have played if I'd been fit. No disrespect to them as well, but the two subs that day were Steve Sedgley and Graham Rodger, two 19-year-old lads, and I would at least have been on the bench and got a winner's medal.

I finished playing because of that hip injury. So I went into managing at 28 at Bilston Town, then, after four years there, went to Stafford Rangers and won the league to get up into what would now be the Conference North level. Those were a great four years there, which I really enjoyed. I had to leave the club because I really needed to get my injury sorted out. It turned out that what I needed was actually the same operation that Roy Keane had. My sciatic nerve was trapped and had caused me all those problems. Phil Robinson, who I'd just signed from Stoke, took over from me at Stafford and he's done a wonderful job getting them back into the Conference.

I managed Hednesford Town after I recovered from my operation, but didn't enjoy it quite as much as I had at Stafford, so left after a year. I'm still only 42 now, but I've managed for over ten years already and got a lot of experience. I can talk the hind leg off a donkey, which I think is why I have been successful as a manager.

BUT THEN, LAST year, I got hit with a huge blow. I had a stroke, which has taken me nearly nine months to recover from. I didn't know what had hit me at first and I was in hospital for weeks, but I am now making a good recovery. I've got a long way to go, but I hope to be back to top form soon.

Talking about my greatest moment as a Stoke player has helped bring the memories flooding back and when you consider that I didn't know what I could and couldn't remember when I agreed to do the interview, I'm so pleased at how much I have been able to recall and I hope that it gives Stokies as much pleasure to remember that great win over a great team as it does me.

IAN CRANSON: BORN 2 JULY 1964, EASINGTON; 279 GAMES, 12 GOALS

Ian Cranson

Liverpool 2 Stoke City 2

League Cup second round first leg

Wednesday 25 September 1991

I WAS AT Stoke for eight years as a player and played over 250 games for the club, so it was difficult to choose just one. There were so many great games.

I imagine that many people would have expected me to select that fantastic match against West Brom at the start of the 1992/93 season which started our push for promotion that year. That was a hell of a game; open and attacking. There were goals flying in all over the place – first it was 1-0 to them, then 2-1 to us, then 3-2 to them. It was crazy – although not from a defender's point of view! Tony Parks made his debut in goal for us and gifted Albion their opening goal when he scuffed a goal kick straight to Bob Taylor.

At 3-3, it looked as though we weren't going to get the result, but I was fortunate to score the winning goal at the Boothen End with a header from a corner. It was a very important result. I think frustration would have set in if we hadn't won that game, but because we did, it lifted what had been an average start to the season and we went on that club record unbeaten run of 25 games which saw us win the Championship that year.

But, great though that game was, I've chosen another special match and special occasion as my game.

THE LEAGUE CUP doesn't always get taken tremendously seriously by supporters and sometimes players, although, of course, it does depend upon who you're playing. That season we'd been drawn against Chesterfield in the first round, which was nothing remarkable, and so less than 8,000 saw the home leg, which we won 1-0 and only 5,000 were at the away leg, which we won 2-1 to progress 3-1 on aggregate. But then you get thrown in with the big teams and we got the most fantastic second round draw when we pulled Liverpool out of the hat. When you get a tie like that you are talking about it from the minute it is drawn right up to the day of the game.

Liverpool had been the team to beat throughout my career, both at Ipswich and Sheffield Wednesday, before I came to Stoke. From the era of Rush and Dalglish, through the likes of Beardsley and Barnes, to this new team, now managed by Graeme Souness. I had never actually beaten them at Anfield, but I had drawn there, although I had also been on the end of a 5-1 drubbing, so there was this little bit of intrepidation as I was not quite sure as to how it was going to be. You're hoping that you can justify doing well on those occasions with a good performance and I knew that anything we took out of the game back to Stoke for the second leg was a bonus.

From my point of view, I thought I'd be happy coming away being able to say to myself that we'd done well as a team and I had done well individually and we'd emerged from it with some credit, but as it turned out we gave them a right game that night. We really pushed them.

Souness was expected to produce big things. He'd only just taken over, but he was Liverpool through and through. He'd been extremely successful at Rangers and people thought he'd be able to bring the kind of total dominance that the team he'd captained to so many trophies in the Eighties had exercised.

Liverpool took the home leg fairly seriously, although there were one or two changes in their side. Reserve Mike Marsh played in midfield and Nicky Tanner at centre-back, but they did have the likes of Dean Saunders, Ian Rush, Steve Nicol, Steve McManaman, Steve McMahon and Ronny Rosenthal in their side. In this day and age big clubs play their reserve side all the way to the final – just look at Arsenal.

IT WASN'T A particularly big crowd by Liverpool's standards. Instead of their usual 40,000 gate, there were only 18,000 there – and at least 6 or 7,000 were Stokies, packing the away end and making a tremendous amount of noise. I think I'm right in saying that they actually gave us extra tickets for that first leg, so when we ran out, on our left hand side it was all Stoke. The atmosphere was great.

Lou had only had a few weeks with us to make a difference and his methods were just beginning to get us fit enough to be able to outrun and outwork opponents. As soon as he came to the club he'd changed the training regime, so we were running a lot and days off became a rarity. We'd never get two in a row. We worked very hard. What most clubs would call a training session Lou would term a loosening session!

Every time he turned up at the training ground we thought, "Oh, here we go again!" He would stop training to make a point, or pull individuals out of the training session to get them to do some running work, or some sprint work. It was tough and there was a bit of moaning, but I think Lou quite liked that. We were an experienced group of players, so we knuckled down as we felt we had massively underperformed in the two previous seasons, which I probably don't have to remind anyone saw the club relegated from Division Two and then finish in mid-table in Division Three. I think we saw this as an opportunity to show what we were really capable of.

I think we'd been a bit lax in our approach to training and games under the previous manager and we were looking for some guidance and a firm hand and that's what Lou supplied. I think he knew what he had to do when he took the job. He knew he had good players. He'd done his background history on us and knew we'd underachieved, and so felt he could bring us up to the level we should be performing at bearing in mind the standard some of the players had played at before. He reduced his tolerance as to what we could get away with and we responded to that and the rest, as they say, is history.

I WAS PARTNERED with Vince Overson in the centre of our defence. Vince had only just joined the club from Birmingham the previous month, where he had worked with Macari. He was a great captain and a good organiser from the back. He was a real character, who had undergone something of a conversion under Lou at St

Andrew's. Vince had slimmed down, become more dominating as a centre-half and captained the club to victory in Autoglass Trophy win in 199??. I don't think he'd achieved what he was capable of until Lou had got there and he'd then had his best years of his career. So he was already a Lou disciple and he was a real influence in the dressing room. To be fair he moaned as much as anyone else about the training, but then he'd been used to it and seen the benefit of it for two years at Birmingham.

Our task that night was to deal with one of the greatest goalscorers of all time in Ian Rush. I'd had problems with him before. He was one of those players that wouldn't do anything for 89 minutes and then would pop up and score a goal, just when you thought you'd had a good game against him. He was a phenomenal striker. You'd look back at the game and think, "Actually I played well," but he'd still have scored a goal.

Perhaps inevitably, Rush scored their first goal that night. Looking back I don't remember him having too many other chances apart from the two he stuck in the back of the net. As I say, he would do that. Lou had decided to play three centre-halves that night, so Lee Sandford was tucked in alongside me and Vince, and I played in a sort of sweeping role, behind the other two. That meant Lee Fowler was drafted in to play on the left hand side of defence. Lee was a young player, who never quite made the step up into the first team, but he did well enough that night. He was up against a young Steve McManaman and did OK against him. Vince had been designated to mark Liverpool's new record signing Dean Saunders, and snuffed him out to the extent that he was substituted. We felt we were doing OK with this formation, and it also allowed me the security to go forward for free kicks knowing that we had numbers at the back to deal with any breakaways.

That's how I scored my goal. Ian Scott took a corner and I just got in front of Steve Nicol six or seven yards out in front of the Kop – which was nice – and it flew into the net. It was a good solid header and that gave us a bit of belief that we could get something out of this match. As much as it helped us, that goal shook them and showed them we were now really up for it. As the game went on we realised we could get a result. We weren't there to be the whipping boys and make the fixture up, we were there to give them a game and take it to their crowd.

Rush got a second goal with about 20 minutes to go, slotting home another classic striker's finish. He was deadly in those situations. But we didn't allow ourselves to get downhearted and kept doing what we'd been doing well. The performance had given us a lot of faith.

Anfield can be a terrifying place where players can be destroyed. I remember as an Ipswich player going there in the quarter-final of the FA Cup and being hammered 3-0. Terry Butcher, who was the England centre-half and obviously a bit of a legend, was at fault for two of the goals and so for the rest of the game the Kop were shouting, "Give it to Butcher. Give it to Butcher." That's how cutting they can be.

Then I went there with Ipswich after we'd beaten Spurs at home on a Saturday. It was a Bank Holiday weekend, so we went to Anfield on the Monday feeling very confident and got spanked 5-1. That was a long 90 minutes and so to have played so well for Stoke was brilliant.

TO BE HONEST I think we'd have been happy to have lost narrowly 2-1, but of course, it got a lot better than that. Tony Kelly's goal is probably one of the most famous Stoke goals ever. Not only was it a last minute equaliser at Anfield, but he nutmegged Bruce Grobbelaar in front of hordes of ecstatic Stokies. He'd latched on to a long ball in our left channel and Gary Ablett, who was playing centre-back, came across, but made a mistake challenging him and allowed Tony to get away. Tony was a head down, pin your ears back type of player. He had real pace, but his finishing was erratic at times, so you never knew what was going to happen. Alan Ball had signed him from non-league St. Albans City. His pace could frighten people and he was capable of doing things that would make you think, "Where did that come from?" He was often used as a sub in a game where players were tiring and his pace could be used well and that's exactly what happened at Anfield. He came on for Tony Ellis up front with a few minutes remaining and buzzed around trying to make a nuisance of himself and get amongst the Liverpool defenders.

So Tony went through and put the ball through Grobbelaar's legs. As I say it was in front of our supporters and that was just a fitting end to the game as they'd stayed with us all match and sung their hearts out for us. I remember this unbelievable Delilah coming down off the stands engulfing Anfield! It was truly memorable.

That's what sticks in my mind, the noise that the fans made. Anfield is a very intimidating place to go for a visiting team, but their home crowd had basically snubbed the game, thinking it would be a walkover, so we had at least 40 per cent of the crowd. To hear the noise throughout the game was great and to finish it off like that was fantastic. It was nice to go to one of the big cathedrals of English football and get a result. I won once at Old Trafford, but never did at Liverpool.

THAT GAME WAS the first time we really clicked as a team and it was the foundation for what turned out to be an incredible season really. I remember when I got home after the game, Lou had done an interview on the TV, and said that the main thing as far as he was concerned was to keep the game alive so that we could take them on in front of a bumper crowd. Well, we'd certainly done that. We'd given ourselves a great chance.

The second leg crowd was over 22,000 and it really gave us a taste of what success could bring. When it was buzzing, the Vic was a hell of a place to play. I remember my debut, which was on the opening day of the 1989/90 season when we drew 1-1 with West Ham, and the place was rocking. Then there were sell-outs for the games against Port Vale, who were on the crest of a wave, so these were the first derby games for 30-odd years. They were fantastic occasions and the atmosphere at the Vic was as good as playing in the First Division. The season before I signed for Stoke I'd been at Sheffield Wednesday in the top flight, playing in front of 30,000, but the atmosphere at the Vic was comparable because it was jumping.

I used to like night games anyway as they had a special atmosphere, with the lights on and a sense of real anticipation, but against Liverpool, although the crowd were up for it, we never quite got in touch with them after they'd scored after ten minutes when

Steve McManaman netted. We went two down when Tony Kelly's back pass found Ian Rush, who set up Dean Saunders for a tap in, but we got back into the game when Bertie scored a penalty after Tanner handled on the line. I came off with fifteen minutes to go as Lou wanted to put another striker on and Liverpool made the game safe when Mark Walters tapped in, but Bertie grabbed a consolation late goal to make it 3-2 on the night and 5-4 to Liverpool on aggregate.

We were never really in it because they'd had their wake-up call at Liverpool and you could see what it meant to them. I remember sitting on the bench and watching how irate Graeme Souness was becoming more and more irate. Whilst they felt comfortable at 2-0, once we pulled one goal back he was not happy as he knew if we scored again they'd be in trouble. And when we pulled it back to 3-2 with a few minutes left, he was screaming and bawling at his players. He was very vocal and aware that this was a potential banana skin. I could see him worrying about what had happened in the first leg when we'd scored that late, late equaliser. He didn't want that happening again. He was already under pressure because they were only mid-table in the league and he'd spent a bit of money and there were question marks hanging over him. You don't expect to be knocked out over two legs by a team two divisions below you. You certainly shouldn't. One-off games are different.

In fact Liverpool struggled against lower league teams that season. They only just got past the Vale in the next round, but lost to Peterborough in the quarter-final. So they had a vulnerable streak in them. They actually won the FA Cup that year, but had a fairly easy draw all the way and beat Second Division Sunderland in the final.

AS THE RESULTS started to turn for us after that we began to think we were doing something right. We'd only won a couple of games up to then, but after the Liverpool matches we only lost one game in the next dozen or so and climbed the table. We'd got some belief that what we were doing was good and bringing results.

It's incredible how much of the game is based on confidence and the mental side of things. Belief and desire are key to being successful and sometimes that can turn on one result. Suddenly a last minute equaliser at Anfield had us thinking, "Eh up. This could be the luck that starts us."

I coach at the Stoke Academy now at under-12 level and we play the likes of Liverpool and it's amazing when the kids turn round after losing 2 or 3-0 and say that they knew that was going to happen. I ask them, "Let's be honest. How many people thought you were going to win today?" And no one put their hands up. So I said, "There you go. You were a beaten team before you even went on that pitch." It's just getting that mentality right. They see Liverpool as this big club, which intimidates them. By the same token, against lesser clubs like Manchester City, they look different players because they feel they can win those games. While it shouldn't matter to the same degree to the senior players, it still has a bearing.

ONE OF THE other big factors, of course, in our success in 1991/92 was the signing of Mark Stein. Steino typified what we had been until Lou began to turn us around. His career was stumbling, he was going nowhere and had become a bit disillusioned with life at Oxford. He was nowhere near fit and you could see in his initial month's loan spell that he hadn't got the sharpness which had made him such a dangerous striker as a youngster with Luton. He didn't score until he signed permanently, but you could see as he was playing more and more he was becoming sharper and he developed a great partnership with Wayne Biggins. The success we had that season was based on that strike partnership, with two forwards who were capable of scoring 20 goals.

We should have got promotion that season. I think we threw it away a bit in the end. We lost a few home games which should have been bankers – against Hull, Chester and Bury. We'd done the hard work to a degree as we'd pegged back Birmingham and beat them in early January to go top, but we blew up a little bit. So we went into the play-offs not as the form team against a difficult Stockport side.

We lost the away leg 1-0, but the big killer was that they scored in the first minute of the second leg at the Vic. Even though Steiny scored with ten minutes to go, we couldn't score again and we went out. That was shattering. We hadn't played well in the two games and I don't think we deserved to go through over those two matches, even though we'd been much the better team over 46 games.

MUCH AS OUR success had been sparked by the arrival of Stein, we had a great back four that was the foundation of what we achieved over the next few seasons. John Butler was one of the best full-backs I played alongside. He was very fit and a good defender and reliable; he didn't miss many games and certainly didn't have many bad matches. He could deliver a good ball into the box and I thought he was capable of playing at a higher level.

Lee Sandford was one of the few Alan Ball signings who made himself a success at Stoke. He had come into a struggling team and never really stamped his authority on the side. Lou got the best out of him, I think. When he was fully fit, Lee's ability came out. He was also consistent, comfortable at full-back and centre-half and he was a lot quicker than people thought. They used to say that the four of us were not particularly quick, but because we were good readers of the game we didn't get exposed very often.

Micky Kennedy played in midfield in those Liverpool games. He played very well that night and had a running battle with McMahon. They both had a reputation, although I think that Mick's overshadowed his ability to play. He was another Ball signing, but for the first part of that 1991/92 season he began to show he had real ability. Alongside him was Carl Beeston, who was a player who had the ability to dominate the game. He was a great passer of the ball, but he needed someone to pester him to get the best out of him and that's what Macari did. Carl could sometimes carry weight and that affected him when he did, but under Macari that wasn't an issue and so he was able to perform to the best of his ability.

WE PLAYED OVER 60 games all told in 1991/92, partly because we had a good run to the final of the Autoglass Trophy at Wembley. I'd only played at the Twin Towers once before in the Football

League Centenary tournament in 1988 for Sheffield Wednesday. That was actually the first time I did my knee, playing against Crystal Palace in one of the opening games. That knee injury would pester me for the remainder of my career, so it was good to lay that particular ghost by emerging victorious from Wembley.

To be honest the Autoglass was a competition we didn't really bother about until we got to the semi-final against Peterborough. Then we had a live Sky game for the first leg of that tie, which ended 3-3. Kevin Pressman had a nightmare in goal that night, so Lou brought Foxy in from the cold to play in the remaining games. I remember being in the dressing room having won 1-0 at Peterborough and the atmosphere was tremendous. We were shouting and cheering, "We're all going to Wembley!" That sort of thing.

It was great to win at Wembley on what was a hot, hot day, but ultimately I suppose Peterborough had the last laugh by getting promotion through the play-offs that year, which left a bit of a sour taste.

It was a wonderful day out, though, and the main thing I remember is seeing all this red and white ringed around Wembley from the Royal Box all the way round two thirds of the stadium, because Stockport had brought so few fans in comparison to Stoke. When we walked up the steps I was looking for my wife in the stands and so I actually missed Vince lifting the cup! I was looking round and all of a sudden there was this big cheer going up! And I still didn't see her!!

When we came back to the Potteries the next day it was still glorious sunshine, as it had been at Wembley, and we got onto the open-topped bus around Rough Close, and there wasn't really anyone there. But as we got to the Windmill pub at Meir, it was packed all the way through the city. Then to finish off at the King's Hall was tremendous. It just blew us away the number of people who turned up.

I remember when the lads won the Autoglass for the second time in 2000 and it peed down with rain all day and no one really turned out to greet the players. I'd been telling them all about how we'd had thousands upon thousands there to celebrate with us, but theirs was a damp squib.

LOU WANTED US to play a no frills game. He didn't want the back four playing it around and passing it short into midfield. He liked to play it forward early. My job as a centre-half was to win the ball and to ensure the opposition didn't get near our goal. It didn't stop us playing when we felt we could, sometimes to Lou's frustration! He saw Stein's pace as a great weapon to hurt opponents with and he wanted to put pressure on the opposing defence rather than simply retain possession in deep lying areas. But as a group of players we liked to express ourselves and I think a lot of teams underrated us as they thought we were merely a long ball team, when we were better than that. And that's why I think we stepped up into the higher division without too many problems after winning promotion in 1992/93.

We had two seasons in mid-table in the Second Division where we could have got involved in the play-offs, but didn't have enough up front, and then the third season we should have gone up really. That was where the financial side of things came into play. We met Leicester in the play-offs and they spent £1.5m on transfer deadline day, while we sold Pesch (Paul Peschisolido), who was one of our three main strikers. Leicester beat us in the play-off semi-final, went on to establish themselves in the Premiership and then began to win things. Then all of a sudden you get the bitter taste, because we thought we wouldn't get a better opportunity that that and we've been proved right. I am convinced that if we'd been braver as a club then we'd have had a bit if success. It rankles a bit. It should have been us, but that's football isn't it?

That season also had a game which sparked us into action like the Liverpool cup tie in 1991 and the West Brom game in 1992. On this occasion we won 1-0 at Premiership Chelsea, who had Ruud Gullit, Dennis Wise and Mark Hughes in their line-up, in the second round of the League Cup. We played really well defensively that night and nicked it when Pesch won possession in the middle of their half, beat a defender, drew the goalkeeper, Dmitri Kharine, and put the ball in the net. Thank you very much. It showed what he was capable of that and we missed his ability to score those kind of goals after he'd been sold. It may have been that he would only have come on from the bench because by the end of the season we had a great strike partnership of Mike Sheron and Simon Sturridge up front, but ten years later Pesch is still coming off the bench to score vital goals, so I think it would have stood us in good stead if we could have kept him.

We deserved that win and the result showed us we could compete with teams from a division higher. It's a big thing with cup games, and it was proved with that Liverpool win as well, that the results can make a huge difference to how your season pans out.

For me that draw at Anfield was the first beginnings of our success under Macari, and it gave me some memories I'll never ever forget.

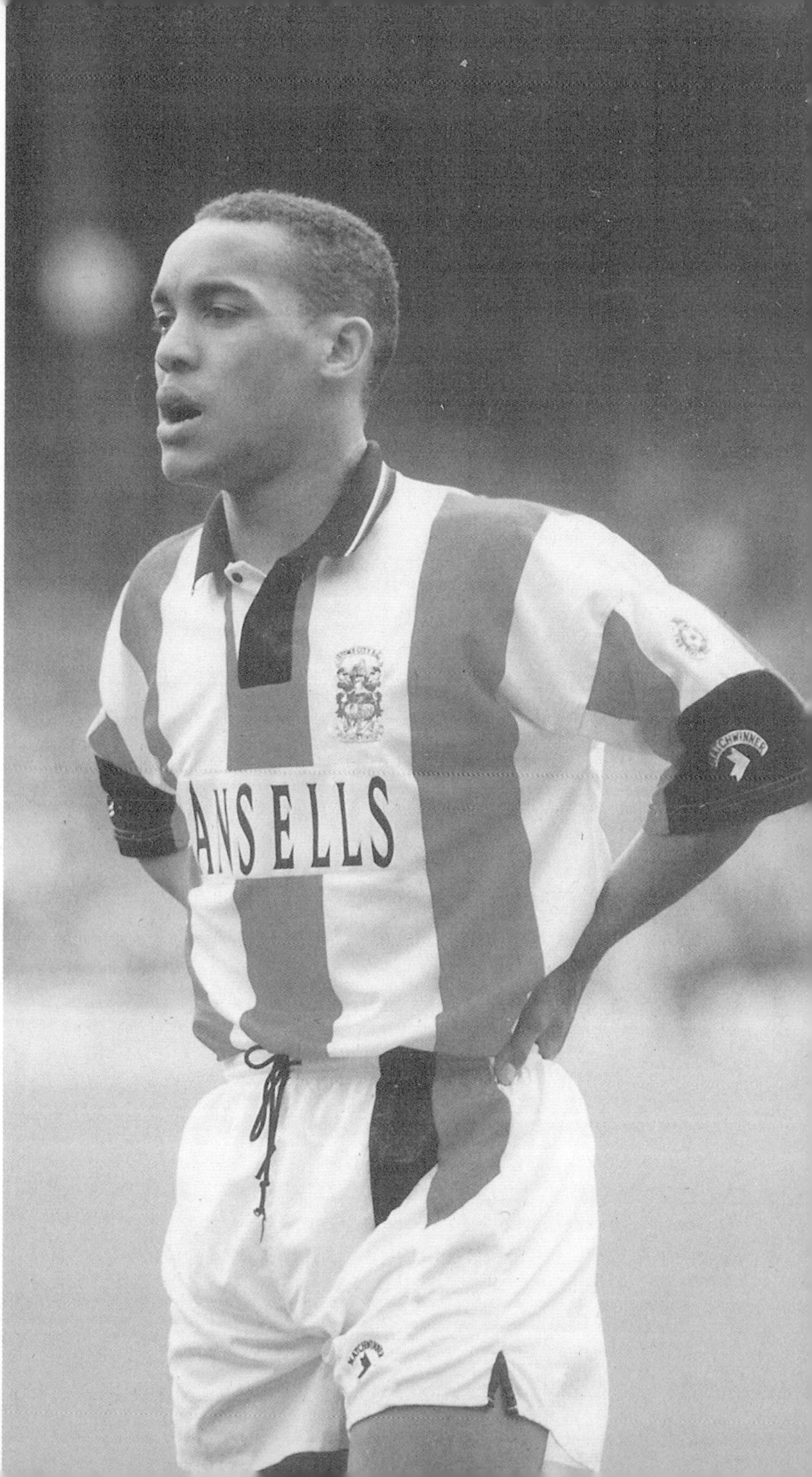

MARK STEIN: BORN 28 JANUARY 1966, CAPE TOWN; 132 GAMES, 71 GOALS

Mark Stein

Stoke City 2 Manchester United 1
League Cup second round first leg
Wednesday 22 September 1993

WHEN THE BALL hit the back of Peter Schmeichel's net it felt like the whole roof lifted off the Victoria Ground. Whoosh! It doesn't get any better than that.

It was always such a great atmosphere down at the Vic because everyone was so close in, right on the touchline. It was a very intimidating place for visiting sides. Lou Macari always emphasised that. He kept saying to us, "make it a fortress." And I believe that in the two and a half years I was there, we did exactly that. It was a fearsome place for teams to come to – even the likes of Manchester United.

Night matches at the Vic were always fantastic occasions, with a real big atmosphere. They felt special. I had to choose beating Manchester United in the League Cup for my game. The place was buzzing with electricity that night and to score the two goals which won the game against the biggest club in the world was incredible.

I first came to Stoke on loan in September 1991 because I was stagnating at Oxford United where I had been in and out of the team. Lou Macari had liked me as a player since I was at Luton at the start of my career. That's why it all transpired. He enquired and the Oxford manager, Brian Horton, allowed me to go. The funny thing was that, although I played well and the team began to get some good results, I didn't actually score a goal during that month's loan. In fact looking at the stats for that time I've now realised that I must have spent the whole month setting 'Bertie' Biggins up for goals, because he scored seven in the five games I played! Seriously though, the players did appreciate what I brought to the team in terms of movement and pace up front.

During that month, I built up a good rapport with Bertie and I did actually make quite a few of those goals. For any striker, if you don't score yourself, you want your partner to find the net. My goal was always set for the team, not for myself, so I was quite happy with my contribution during that loan period and the players were too and certainly the manager must have been because he paid £100,000 for me to sign permanently. As it turns out that may have been a bit of a steal for Stoke considering they sold me two years later for £1.2m!

Actually I don't think Wayne was a player who got as much credit as he probably should. He was a good goalscorer, but perhaps because he left early in the promotion season, that's why Stoke fans have mixed feelings about him. He was a really good player and we complemented each other very well.

Lou Macari fostered a good team spirit amongst the squad, which made us bond well together and we were very strong both physically and mentally.

We won a lot of games in that season and led the table for much of it, but he would never let us get carried away and we would always go out there and run our socks off for 90 minutes. There weren't any real stars in the team, although obviously Bertie and I were the strikers and got all the plaudits for scoring the goals, but it was a good unit and without the other players us forwards would have been nothing really.

That first season we had been top of the league for several months after Christmas and we blew our chance of promotion really. Most of us hadn't been in that position before of being on top and having to get across the winning line. We lost three stupid home games against Bury, Hull and Chester, which cost us dearly and we never really recovered from the shock of ending up in the play-offs and not going up automatically. It devastated us actually.

In the play-offs we met our bogey team, Stockport. They were very much a long ball team with this enormous centre forward, Kevin Francis (6ft 7in), who was probably the most opposite kind of player to me that there was in football. They were a really big team throughout that relied on their height and strength. We went to Stockport for the first leg of the play-off semi-final and it turned into a nightmare really. Carl Beeston got all het up about a bad foul on Bertie Biggins by their player Lee Todd and flattened the guy and got himself sent off. It was never a sending off really. It was crazy. Their players did very well to encourage the referee to send him off knowing that Beest was one our big players. We really missed him in the second leg. Then they scored a free kick to win the first game 1-0. The second leg started horrendously; the ball bobbled around our box and was headed in by Chris Beaumont and then we had to throw caution to the wind and attack. We bombarded them for the entire 89 minutes, but however hard we tried we only got one goal back – when I scored with a few minutes to go – and we were out. Perhaps it wasn't meant to be. We always felt we had better individual players than them and in fact I think six of our players got into the PFA divisional team at the end of the season.

They'd caught us at a time when we were below our best because we'd failed to go up automatically. But the good news was that we had an instant opportunity for revenge. We wanted to prove that we were the better team that year and the Autoglass Trophy final just three days later gave us the chance. It was an incredible day. Stoke hadn't been to Wembley for 20 years and the support we got was out of this world. As we travelled to Wembley it seemed that every car we saw had Stoke fans crammed into it and there were about 40,000 supporters in the ground. To score the only goal was amazing. I remember Adrian Heath won a free kick and it was played into their box and headed away, but it fell to Lee Sandford who flicked it over the top of the Stockport defence for me to run on to. I think some of them were calling for offside, but I didn't worry as I was concentrating on my shot. I struck the ball well and fortunately it went in to the top corner.

After that we knew we had the game won and I thought they were a beaten team. Probably their only chance would have been from a set piece, but we dominated the rest of the game. It was incredibly hot and Stockport's game was based on power and pace, pumping long balls and running after them and I think they ran themselves to a standstill that day.

Due to us losing out on promotion, we were so determined not to go away empty-handed and to send all those fans home happy after seeing them so sad on the previous Wednesday was fantastic. The goal lives on in my mind as clear as day, and I very nearly chose this game as my favourite because you don't score at Wembley, especially a winning goal, very often. It was justice, I thought, that we won that game as it gave us something to end that great season on a high with.

But we then had to get ourselves up for the beginning of the 1992/93 season. The good thing was we didn't have a hangover from the previous season. If we hadn't won at Wembley maybe we'd have crumbled mentally, but you could see from the word go on everyone's faces that as a group we were so determined to win promotion that year, to show we were the best team in the league. We worked doubly hard, which when you're being trained by Lou Macari is very hard I can tell you! Everyone was extremely fit and, don't forget, we had good players throughout the team. We also faced a problem in that being the biggest club in the division, we had all the other clubs seeing us as their cup final that year. They loved to try and take us on as we were the team to beat.

We actually started quite slowly, but went on a run of unbeaten games that set a new club record and effectively won us promotion. We did have a few hairy moments along the way. I remember the day that we beat Orient at home, and I missed a penalty just on half-time as well, didn't I? But I managed to make amends with two goals in the last five minutes after Orient had taken the lead. That dramatic win moved us into the top half of the table in early October for the first time and we didn't look back from there. That was actually the first win of 11 from 12 games as we began to fly.

One of the major reasons for our success was that Lou added Kevin Russell into the mix and he added something different because he could get past people on the wing and get to the byline to send over crosses. We started scoring on a regular basis and every time we went out we thought we were going to score lots of goals. We knew things would happen. It was such a good season because we could overpower teams.

The supporters played a huge role in that. I've always said that Stoke supporters have been through so many lulls and disappointments that they deserve success. It's such a huge club and all they want is for their players to show passion. Once you put on that red and white shirt they demand you show some desire and give your all for the club. They travelled everywhere for us that season; Hartlepool, Brighton, Exeter, Hull, Chester, all sorts of places. They are the best supporters by far of any that I have ever had the pleasure of playing for. I can't tell you how special they were. And thank you to all those who supported me and the team. You really helped us win promotion that season.

We clinched the title and promotion on the same night when we beat Plymouth. There were three games to go and we needed just three points to make sure. I nearly selected this game as my match as well, but really I suppose it was Peter Fox's night as he'd been at the club for so long and he made that magnificent double save from Warren Joyce to keep us 1-0 ahead. That won us the game really.

It was such a great night, but the game itself was very nerve-wracking. You could sense in the changing room beforehand what it meant. We didn't want the same thing to happen as had the year before, so we were nervous and we didn't play well because of that. Fortunately for us we saw the game out and won thanks to Nigel Gleghorn's early goal. It was a great feeling when the final whistle went and all the fans began jumping around on the pitch. There must have been 20,000 on there going crazy. It was madness. I don't think we left the ground until about 12 o'clock and even then there were supporters milling around outside. It was a truly great night.

The other game from that season that was in the running for my match was the 2-0 win at Port Vale in the league. Scoring at Vale Park was incredible. Obviously the Vale fans gave me untold abuse and made me feel very welcome after that! I scored really early in the game, lashing home the ball in a goalmouth scramble. It was a filthy night, but the crowd was over 20,000. It felt like most of them were Stokies. I remember when I scored the whole of that end went loopy. That was a big, important game for us as it was in the run in to the Championship season and Vale were one of our main promotion rivlas.

The Stoke Vale rivalry was incredibly intense at that point. I remember my first derby, when we won 2-1 at the Vic and I won a late penalty, which Vale hotly disputed to put it mildly. As I put the ball down on the spot, Peter Swan walked past me and said, "Let's see how your bottle is." That kind of stuff is just part and parcel of the game and you have to learn to cope with it. So I scored the penalty, which we knew would win us the game, and ran back to the halfway line past Swanny and said, "Fine, thank you. Not too bad at the moment."

Strangely we won promotion from Division Two to Division One not from Three to Two because the creation of the Premiership meant the leagues were renamed. We had come up into this new division and everyone was wondering how we were going to do because Lou didn't add that many players to the squad. He basically went with the same team. The main addition was Icelandic international midfielder Toddy Orlygsson from Nottingham Forest.

Funnily enough, another game I thought about picking was our 3-2 victory at Forest which really put us on the First Division map as we were finding our feet in the new league. We'd just won up at Middlesbrough, who were promotion favourites and our next game was at the home of the other promotion favourites, Forest. The game was live on ITV and we had a stormer.

We went to the City Ground as the massive underdogs as in their team they had Stuart Pearce, Stan Collymore, Mark Crossley and Steve Stone – all established names. Lou always used to tell us on these occasions that we were a rag, tag and bobtail team, who the likes of Forest did not think have any right to be there. As you can see, he was always complimenting us!

Needless to say he was winding us up, and we didn't fear anyone. That's what was so good about us. We didn't have any mental deficiencies. We were always confident that if we worked hard as a unit we would be alright and so it didn't matter where we played. I actually remember that when we got back into the changing room after we'd won that we weren't all giving it, "We've beaten Nottingham Forest." We were actually quite calm about it because we expected to be able to pull off results like that because we fancied ourselves so strongly. And if you have that mental strength you can attain almost anything I believe.

We took the lead thanks to a Dave Regis goal. Dave was a bustling, big lad, but he was also fast because he was related to John Regis the British Olympic sprinter, and he and I were a handful for Forest that day. I scored a penalty, although it wasn't the best penalty, as it only just went under Crossley's body as he dived. But it went in for 2-0. And then Micky Gynn slipped a ball through to me and it sat up nicely on the volley about 18 yards out, but it was on my left foot, not my favoured right. Now my left foot was mostly for standing on, but on this occasion the ball floated in over Crossley. Forest came back and made it 3-2 in the end, but we played really well that day and that gave us confidence for this massive game we had coming up.

In the first round of the League Cup we had been paired with Mansfield and we'd had a bit of a dodgy game in the first leg at the Vic. We drew 2-2 at home after being 2-1 down. Then we couldn't finish them off in the away leg and drew 1-1 over the 90 minutes, but just into extra time I managed to score and that knocked the stuffing out of them. They tired and we outlasted them to win 3-1 on the night in the end.

That sent us into the hat for the second round and we drew out Manchester United. Not only were they top of the Premiership at the time, packed with megastars like Bryan Robson, Mark Hughes, Peter Schmeichel and Gary Pallister, they also happen to be the biggest club in the world – and my team. I'd supported United since I was a boy. And, of course, the Stoke manager, Lou Macari had played for United. In fact he'd been in the team that I grew up with that won the 1977 FA Cup Final by beating Liverpool.

Everyone wants to draw Manchester United in any cup competition and for us to do so was fantastic. The ground was sold out and it was one of those magical nights at the Vic. You always want to pit yourself against the best and Alex Ferguson picked a strong side. Having just won promotion we really fancied giving them a good game. To be honest he didn't leave too many players out, only Bruce, Giggs and Keane. Certainly if you look at the teamsheet, Schmeichel was in goal, Robson played, Pallister,

Hughes, Kanchelskis, McClair, Irwin. They were all fantastic players. That night the crowd was anticipating an upset. You could taste it in the air. From the changing rooms at the Vic you could hear the crowd outside and before the game that night it was truly amazing. Even when we were running out we could feel the buzz. You can't put that feeling into words.

And then the place exploded when I scored the first goal. I can't remember who passed me the ball, but I got it on the right hand side of the penalty area. All I was thinking about was trying to get a shot off really. I ran at Pallister and hit it on the run and it dipped over Schmeichel and clattered into the stanchion inside the net and I thought, "Blimey. I didn't realise I could do that! Lucky me! I can't be that bad a player!"

That raised the roof a bit, but it was only a prelude to what was to happen when the winning goal went in. We got well and truly stuck into United and didn't give them any time on the ball. Let's face it, if you give players like that time they are going to murder you. You could be embarrassed really because they have so much ability.

Dion Dublin equalised totally against the run of play. Lee Sharpe put the ball across and Dublin rose above the defence to head home. But fair play to us, we didn't get downhearted. It didn't really knock us out of our stride.

We just thought, "It's only 1-1."

And the fans kept with us. Of course in the second half we were kicking towards the Boothen End and just a few minutes after Dublin's equaliser, I struck this lucky shot! I don't mean lucky in the sense that I mishit it or anything, but lucky in that to hit two screamers like that in the same game is unusual; for me anyway! It was one of those things that on that night I was fortunate because I hit two fantastic shots that flew in. It was my lucky night. And, of course, that second one was into the Boothen End net. I didn't have a goal celebration. I just used to love watching the Boothen go absolutely crazy. That night the place was rocking. There was something special about it. To me to see that sea of people happy was fantastic. To me the fans gave me as much pleasure as I gave them. I always carried it with me that they followed us everywhere giving us support and I wanted to give them something to cheer. I wanted to show what they meant to us and what winning for Stoke meant to us.

To beat the greatest club in the world was fantastic. We had pitted our wits against the best team in the Premiership, with most of their first team playing and we weren't found wanting. We did celebrate that night.

A few of the lads went out into town, but really we were almost straight away focussing on the next game. That was the beauty of that Stoke team; total commitment.

Of course the problem was that this was a two-legged tie. But we had a lead to take to Old Trafford and we didn't get overawed by the occasion. Lou played the whole thing down. In fact as soon as we came off the pitch at the end of the first leg, all he said was, "Remember boys we've got another leg to come." That was Lou. He never went mad over anything.

But don't think it wasn't special for Lou Macari. Remember this was his old club we'd beaten. Deep down he was delighted, believe me!

Old Trafford was amazing and we took a fantastically vocal support up there. I think when you go somewhere like that and a lot of the team haven't played there before, although I had when I was at Luton, it sends a tingle down your spine. You know, when you play in the lower divisions and you're watching places like that on TV and wishing you were there, you have literally dreamed of that moment. You don't get any bigger than Man United at Old Trafford. It was unfortunate that the game went the way it did as we felt we did very well and didn't get overawed. Lee Sharpe scored just after half-time with a cracking volley, when we had planned to keep them out for at least ten minutes to really frustrate them and get the crowd turned on them. But we did well for the remainder of the second half until right at the end when, with five minutes to go, Brian McClair scored from about ten yards to put us out.

Let's be honest. They had better players than us, which is why they were at Man United. It wasn't meant to be, but we had played really well. And that was important as we were in the process of establishing the club back in the First Division. We had shown what we could do and we were just a few minutes away from taking United into extra time. They had shown us even more respect by naming Bruce and Keane in an even stronger line-up for that second leg and Ferguson was forced to bring on Ryan Giggs from the bench to try and break us down in the second half.

NOT LONG AFTER that match, of course, both Lou and I moved on. Like any player I wanted to better myself and play at the best standard I could. Chelsea came in for me and offered me Premiership football. I wanted to play against the Man Uniteds and the Liverpools of this world on a regular basis to see how I fared. I can honestly say I only moved for footballing reasons. You always want to be at the highest level in any job you do and I played in Europe for Chelsea and in cup finals. Lou went to manage Celtic, which was fair enough because they were his club as a boy. He had begun his career there and I think he had to take the offer when it was made to him. It is a huge club, a massive club.

But a club like Stoke City is bigger than any individual. It will always go on no matter who comes and goes, but I always carry a little piece with me in my heart. I always look for their result, no matter where I have been in my career. The times I had at Stoke were very special to me, which is why I came back for a short loan spell around Christmas 1996, because I had enjoyed my time there and the camaraderie and the spirit amongst players and fans was second to none.

I have recently qualified as a Chartered Physiotherapist and am entering the strange world of work. I wanted to give something back after my career ended and so I had to go through going back to school to do my course and have had some experience working at football clubs like Grays Athletic in the Conference. I would love to work at a high level of the game some day, but now I am going through the process of interviews for jobs, which is novel because footballers don't do interviews in that sense! I am hoping to work in hospitals for a while to see the other side of life after spending 20 years playing the game. A few people said I was crazy taking on all the hard work of doing the course, but I find the work so rewarding and it's great to be able to give something back. When you play football everything is structured for you and when you go outside of your little comfort zone it suddenly becomes very difficult. I wanted to break through all that, so I am now looking to develop my new career and I only hope that it's as successful and as enjoyable as my time at the Vic.

MIKE SHERON: BORN 11 JANUARY 1972 ST HELENS; 74 GAMES, 39 GOALS

Mike Sheron

Stoke City 1 Charlton Athletic 0
League Division One
Wednesday 17 April 1996

I SO WANTED Stoke to go up and be a part of the Premiership that I'd tasted for the first three years of my career at Manchester City. I was desperate to win the play-offs in 1996. We'd had a great season, probably my best of my career personally, and I thought we could do it. We really should have done it.

I SIGNED SCHOOLBOY forms at Man City at 14 and then graduated to the two year YTS scheme which they had in operation at the time. The second year I was there we reached the FA Youth Cup final with a side that included a lot of players who went on to have good careers, such as Neil Lennon, Michael Hughes, Ashley Ward and someone Stoke fans might know a little about, Gerry Taggart. We played Watford in the final and got beat 2-1 after extra time. Watford had David James in goal for them. That apprenticeship, playing with those good players set me up for a good career and set my standards high.

Then I graduated to the reserves. I was scoring goals and my confidence was sky high and eventually I went to Bury on loan on transfer deadline day in 1991. Bury were going for the play-offs in the Third Division. My debut was actually the last game of the season and we needed to beat Tranmere away to confirm Bury's place in the play-offs and I scored the goal as we won 1-0.

That meant we had a two-legged semi-final with Bolton, which was a bit of a local derby. Both games were sell-outs and the first leg at Gigg Lane was a 0-0 draw. I didn't do so well in that game. I felt I didn't do myself justice and the City manager Peter Reid was in the stands. But when we played the second leg, City's first team was away, so no one saw me have a great game at Burnden Park. We just lost out 1-0, though, so that was the first piece of heartache I had in the play-offs in my career.

All of a sudden I was thrown into the City first team squad and scored four in the first seven games of the 1992/93 season, playing alongside Niall Quinn and David White in a three-pronged attack. It was an exciting time. Niall would always play centrally, but David and I would swap around depending on where his blistering pace could be used best; sometimes through the middle, but sometimes on the wing. It was a period of my career that I really enjoyed and everything seemed to be going really well. City finished ninth that season with the likes of Ian Brightwell, Tony Coton and Steve McMahon. I always look back on my time there fondly.

MY TIME WAS up at Manchester City when they sacked Peter Reid and brought Brian Horton in. The team was struggling and Horton didn't seem to rate me. He didn't give me any confidence. I'd been doing well for three years and he didn't really give me a chance, preferring to bring his own men in.

I also had a number of injury problems. That was the beginning actually of the injuries which plagued my career. I didn't know what was going on though. I remember having a 20-yard sprint race with Steve McMahon one day and those that remember Steve will know that he wasn't the quickest, and me being a centre-forward, I thought I would beat him easy. But he beat me and I was thinking, "What's going on here?"

I never really found out what the problem was even when I got to Norwich and had four or five hamstring strains down there. I had a horrible time at Carrow Road. I never got fit, never had a run of games. All this was because of my back. It was causing me all these problems and even when I came to Stoke I didn't really get it sorted. It wasn't until I went to QPR that I was sent to Harley Street to see a consultant. That was the benefit of being the club's record signing at £2.6m, I suppose. They made sure they looked after me as well as they could and being in London meant that I had access to the best care there was. My injury finally got fixed by this specialist who realised my back was squeezing on to my spine because of my posture. That gave me sciatica which in turn caused me to have lower back pain and numerous hamstring pulls. I reckon my career would have been ended a lot sooner if it hadn't been for that specialist. I have a lot to thank him for.

But when I came to Stoke, even though I didn't know what the problem was yet, what manager Lou Macari did was get me fit and look after me while I edged my way into the team. It was actually very frustrating for me at the time, because he played me as a substitute for the first half dozen or so games, while I was raring to go. But he knew what he was doing. I scored my first goal for the club as a substitute against Crystal Palace just before Christmas and then started against Sheffield United and scored again. I never looked back after that.

I always put the success we had at Stoke down to the way Macari got us fit. We could compete for the whole 90 minutes. But also he had assembled a team with good all-round attributes. You had the likes of Nigel Gleghorn and Kevin Keen, who were good passers of the ball and could play passes in for me to run on to. Keen was nice and tidy and played good angled passes. Then you had young Graham Potter providing crosses from the left wing. Potter was skin and bone, but had a really good left foot. Although he didn't score many goals, he did create a lot for us up front. Carl Beeston and Ray Wallace had the job of winning the ball and giving it out simply. Beeston was a vastly underrated player for me. He had an eye for a good pass and I thrived on the chances they gave me. We had some very creative footballers and I look back and think I was lucky to play in that team, but you have to make the most of it and we did at that time.

The defence was very solid – too solid sometimes, I thought. Lou Macari didn't like his full-backs going too far forward, which annoyed me at first, but you do begin to appreciate it when you nick one goal and the defence keep a clean sheet and you win 1-0 and the name on the scoresheet is Sheron. That makes you look good as a striker, although obviously the whole team has contributed to winning the game.

Those full-backs Lee Sandford and Ian Clarkson were both very good players. Neither overlapped very much, though. I always thought Lee was a top defender; physically strong and never caught in a compromising position – on the pitch anyway. He was cultured on the ball and later moved to centre-half from left-back.

Initially I didn't really know who I would be playing up front with. There were actually five first team forwards at the club, myself, Simon Sturridge, John Gayle, Paul Peschisolido and Martin Carruthers. I remember this one day Lou dragged us all into his office and said, "Hey lads, I can only pick two of you, maybe three at a push, so please don't be coming and knocking on my door asking why you're not playing." They all had different strengths. Big John Gayle was a brute of a centre-forward who gave us another option if we needed some height. But I made myself into the main man and gradually a partnership with Simon Sturridge developed. When we played alongside each other our movement created space, but then it's what you do with that space and time and it seemed to click with us. We hit it off and we were sharp. We wanted the ball in and around the box to cause problems for the opposition. We had a licence to roam and go and cause havoc for defences.

I didn't have pace to burn, but I could time my runs and get on the end of the precision passes that were coming from midfield. I remember a goal we scored away at Charlton the following season when we broke away from a corner and played three quality balls upfield and then Graham Kavanagh played me in on the near post to sweep the ball high into the net. It was a fabulous move which included a couple of trademark precision passes.

I used to really enjoy playing against Charlton. I always seemed to score against them and I see them in the Premiership now and I think, "That should have been us."

We had some characters around the club as well. There was this bloke called Neil Baldwin who was our kit man. He was hilarious. He'd apparently been a clown earlier in his life and so we all called him 'Nello the clown'. He was a funny feller and it was nice to have him around at times, just to take the pressure off. We used to play tricks on him. He got tied up and left in the changing rooms for one game!

I remember Mark Prudhoe was a very underrated keeper as well. One of the funniest things I ever saw was when we played a friendly up at Carlisle because they were opening a new stand or something in pre-season. We were coming out before the game in dribs and drabs to warm up and Carlisle had this former all-time hero on the pitch and he was getting a tremendous reception with everyone round the ground standing up to cheer. Just at the moment this Carlisle legend was introduced, Mark came down the tunnel on to the pitch and milked the applause as if it was he who was getting it! He turned around and clapped everyone all around the ground, held his thumbs up, everything! It had us in stitches.

THE SEASON WE reached the play-offs we scored a good number of goals and there was a period in that run in to the end of the season when I scored in seven consecutive games. That set a club record which still stands and its one I'm very proud of – although ultimately of course what matters more is that we weren't successful that season.

The strange thing was that the run started and ended against Charlton. They were one of the other main play-off contenders and we lost the game at the Valley 2-1, when we were leading going into the last ten minutes. Then they scored a controversial penalty for Ian Clarkson's handball and David Whyte's header won the game for them. That was quite sickening as we'd have gone above them into fourth place if we'd won, so my goal didn't feel as if it was that important.

Oddly, although everyone remembers my scoring record, no one remembers that we actually lost three of the games. We won the other four, so it wasn't disastrous by any means, but we also lost the next game at Derby, who were chasing Sunderland hard for the title at the top of the table. Again we took the lead away from home and held it at half-time. I remember the old Baseball Ground pitch was terrible after some rain and we pulled off a fantastic break away from a corner for Sturridge to cross from the right and I dived to head home at the far post. But Derby had a very good side including Simon's brother Dean up front and he scored twice as they came back to win 3-1.

We were now only clinging on to the last play-off spot by the skin of our teeth and needed to beat Wolves at home. I scored very early on when I flicked Nigel Gleghorn's goalbound shot past the keeper. You have to claim those when you're a striker! Simon scored a second as we won 2-0. That brought some relief after two disappointing results.

One of the other new players in the Stoke team was central defender Larus Sigurdsson. He'd only arrived at Stoke because his cousin Toddy Orlygsson was playing for the club, having signed from Nottingham Forest. Larus turned up and was put straight into the team by Lou at Portsmouth before Christmas 1994 and he made a central defensive spot his own. He was cool and collected on the ball and could carry it out of defence to turn a sticky situation into attack. That's exactly what he did that night against Wolves when he set up the second goal with a typical run out of defence.

Having got ourselves back on track we then went and blew it a bit by losing at home 2-1 to Grimsby, who were only a lower mid-table side. Yet again I opened the scoring and we led at half-time. This time I scored a bit of a cheeky goal when I back-heeled it past their keeper, who didn't move! I was really pleased with the different types of goals I was scoring. But we conceded two silly goals in the second half to lose a match we should have won.

So we had now dropped out of the play-off spots, but we'd got a couple of games in hand. One of those was at Luton. That was a very memorable match because we played really poorly, yet still came out as winners. Luton were fighting relegation and so began the game in a whirlwind. They scored right on half-time when Kim Grant netted. To be honest they deserved it and we didn't play much better in the second half. With five minutes to go the score was still 1-0 and I think Luton thought they'd got it won.

But then I remember a great ball from Nigel Gleghorn which put Sturridge in for our first goal goal. It was a 50-yard pass that played Simon in to shoot low into the net. And then Gleggy crossed a free kick for me to head home right in front of the away fans. It was an incredible turn around.

I remember after that game being in the bath at Kenilworth Road and Chic Bates, the coach, walking in. He didn't say anything because he was a bit stunned at what we'd done like me, so we just looked at each other and shrugged as if to say, "Can you believe it?" I mean, I hadn't played that well that night at all, but I got on the end of that decent cross from Nige and scored. That's what it's about. We dug in when things were going against us and we came up smelling of roses.

That year I just felt so confident and had now scored in five games in a row. The papers were full of the possibility of a record now (The record of scoring six games in a row was held by the club's record goalscorer and legend John Ritchie), but I honestly just felt that every game I was going out for I was going to score a goal. I just had utter belief in myself and I had utter belief in my team-mates that they were going to create the opportunity for me to score. So as far as I was concerned there was no pressure at all; the opposite in fact. I was really enjoying myself and loving it at the time.

NEXT UP WERE Portsmouth. I don't remember much about that game or my goal, but I do know it was a last minute winner. That kept my run going and I'd now scored six goals in six games. Most importantly we won and our home record in general was what got us into the play-off. We only lost four games all season at the Victoria Ground and I always fancied us to score goals there.

So it was all set up for me to break the record in a rearranged game against Charlton. It was a bit of a nothing game really apart from the fact that we won with my goal that smashed the record. I remember Sturridge flicking the ball over the back four and I turned, latched on to it and had utter concentration on myself and my technique. I hit it just right, with power and direction and I can see me hitting it in my mind's eye now; head low, knee over the ball, clean strike right through it. The second I hit it I just knew in my own mind that it was going into the top corner.

When the ball hit the back of the net there was a moment of stillness and then an explosion; both in the ground and in my own mind. I remember thinking, "This is what football's about." It was an incredible buzz. The Boothen End went mad. I didn't obviously realise it at the time, but I didn't get too many feelings like that in the game. In fact that was most definitely the best. You know, with the Boothen End all singing my name and I felt like the next thing I was going to do was win the World Cup for England. It was just utter ecstasy I suppose. I will always remember that feeling. It didn't ever got bettered in my career, even previously at Man City.

To be honest I don't remember much about the rest of the game at all. In fact I don't think anyone does. What mattered about that match at the time was the three points, but looking back now I still relive that moment because of the very special feeling it gave me.

I REALLY FELT I could keep my run going even in the next game at champions Sunderland. In fact I was devastated that I didn't score at Roker Park. I remember thinking, "Just carry on what you're doing, what you're doing's great," and I felt that things were going for me and so I doubly expected to score a goal. I remember that game being a bore draw on TV and I was gutted not to score. For it to end all of a sudden I came off the cloud, but you know it can't go on forever.

So now we were just a few points off confirming our place in the play-offs and we won the next game at Millwall 3-2 to put us right on the brink. I remember my goal that day clearly. I cut in from the left and whacked it and the ball just flew into the back of the net past Kasey Keller, who was no bad keeper by the way. I enjoyed that goal because I hit it with power and from the edge of the area. I didn't score too many like that, although I do remember another one at Ipswich the following season. Ray Wallace set me up on the left corner of the penalty area and I hit this waist-high volley right into the far top corner of the net. That was a real beauty. Ipswich were another team I enjoyed scoring against. In the play-off season I scored twice in a 3-1 victory over them, another game which sticks in my mind.

I like to think I scored all different types of goals, right foot, left foot, headers, lucky ones and one or two 20 yarders. Not too many penalties, though. I only took one at Stoke and hit the post with it against Palace. You may not know, but I shied away from penalties after that, even though Lou Macari used to encourage me to take them. He wanted his strikers to score goals and it didn't matter how we got them, it built confidence. As it was, Simon Sturridge took on the penalty-taking duties, although we didn't get too many when I was at Stoke. As it was I liked to take free kicks. Again that was something Lou encouraged as he thought I was good on a dead ball. I remember at the start of the following season we began the campaign really well, with four successive wins and were top of the table when we played at Reading and I scored a great free-kick in a 2-2 draw.

To be a striker you have to be multi-talented and be able to go on your left foot if the defender shows you that way. I was never the quickest, the biggest or the strongest, but I was good at everything. I scored goals at the near post and the far post. That's something you have to work on, you have to keep practising.

We always thought we were good enough to get into the play-offs but we didn't confirm it until the last game, which was at home to Southend. That was a very tense day, but I think I settled the nerves a bit by scoring after about ten minutes when I hit a right-footed volley that won us the game. They gave us the odd scare, but we hung on and secured fourth place in the division in the end.

WHEN I KNEW we were playing Leicester City it meant something to me. Their manager was Martin O'Neill, who had left Norwich to take control of Leicester earlier in the season and masterminded their rise up the table and into the play-offs. O'Neill was the manager who had got rid of me at Norwich, although I always have the knowledge that Stoke fans were so grateful to get rid of the striker that was part-exchanged with me that I will always get a good reception! This poor guy's name was Keith Scott and Stokies had had enough of him judging by what I was told. He'd barely scored a goal and missed a few sitters apparently, so I was on a winner from the start!

Anyway Martin had not really given me chance and now here we were playing against him for a place in the Wembley final. I felt we were more than capable of winning the semi-final. We'd beaten Leicester twice that season in the league already and I had the extra motivation of putting one over O'Neill.

We drew the first leg 0-0 at Filbert Street and Simon Sturridge had a one-on-one with their keeper Kevin Poole and then Graham

Potter missed a back-post header from a great cross from about two yards out. Actually he didn't miss as such, Poole made a great save, but he shouldn't have been allowed to save it. We should have scored. I was a bit gutted that nothing fell to me that day as I was really up for it. We were all disappointed that the game only ended 0-0. We should have won.

I had a strange feeling after the game. Obviously we were optimistic that we were coming back to the Vic and we thought, "Come on. We can take these. They're nothing special." But I just had this inkling that we'd had our chance.

In the second leg, just two days later, we didn't play well and we couldn't get the ball off Emile Heskey, who was an up-and-coming centre-forward at Leicester then. We didn't create any chances and it felt like another 0-0. Then this ball came over from the left and their midfielder Garry Parker cracked in a left footed volley into the roof of the net. It was the one moment of real quality in the entire semi-final and I suppose deserved to win the game. But it hurt. It hurt me, it hurt the team and, I believe, it seriously hurt the club.

But what went wrong for me was that in between the two games Lou had us in for training as usual. Bear in mind it was the end of a long season and we'd played 46 games already, so you were either fit or you weren't, you know what I mean? Plus there were only two days between the matches, so we really needed to recover, not train. I know for a fact now that we were worked much harder than them and it disappoints me. I spoke to one of the Leicester players who asked me what we did on the Monday after the first leg on the Sunday and we'd had a full two-hour session, while they came in and stretched for 15 minutes and then went home. And that does disappoint me. I look back and I think we should have been looked after a bit better. It was hard to swallow, I suppose and at the end of the day we lost 1-0 after not playing that well.

There is one thing I would like to mention about that game. One story that no one knows. I hated Martin O'Neill because of the way I felt he treated me at Norwich. He never gave me a chance, although he had his reasons and at the end of the day he just wanted to pick players who were performing for Norwich. I think I had been taken off towards the end of the game and when the final whistle went, I turned and trudged straight down the tunnel. Martin caught up with me and tapped me on the back and I turned round and he said, "I was wrong about you, you know." And that changed my view of him really. When people talk to me about him now I have a bittersweet feeling. Obviously he has gone on and managed some great clubs, and won things and had a great career. But if he hadn't said what he did after that game I would have happily told you how much I hated him and how crap he was! But actually he did say some very nice things that night and I appreciate them. I'm sure that won't help any Stoke City fans get over that disappointment, but it helped me slightly.

ONE OF THE questions Stoke fans always ask me is whether I think the sale of Paul Peschisolido on transfer deadline day was a reason why we didn't go up that year. What I remember of that day is that the club used to have a house just opposite the ground and a few of us were hanging round in it ready to go out that night in town. There were five or six of us, Pesch, Ray Wallace and myself included. It was early evening and Pesch got a phone call to go down to the club. Next thing we heard, next morning, was that he'd gone back to Birmingham to his Mrs! That was all we knew about it. Cloak and dagger stuff, but to be honest it didn't affect us too much. He hadn't been playing in games because Simon and I had done so well, but, of course, he is still proving today that he can be effective as a substitute and come on to exploit tired legs late in games.

WHAT REALLY HURTS now about that defeat, looking back at the end of my career, was that I never got to play at Wembley. I got there with Barnsley in the play-offs one season, but I sat on the bench all game. I won the LDV Vans trophy with Blackpool, but that was at the Millennium Stadium. It's a great place to play football, but it was half empty, and although we won, I didn't have the best game. To play at Wembley with Stoke would have been wonderful. I know it would have been full and rocking with Stoke fans.

Let's face it, Leicester were nothing special. Their midfield was OK; Neil Lennon, Garry Parker and Muzzy Izzett, while they had Steve Claridge and Emily Heskey up front. They had a solid team, but nothing spectacular.

I think we had as good a team as them and it would have been nice to have tried to have a crack at the Premiership as I think myself and Simon Sturridge would have given a lot of defences problems. As it was Leicester went on to win promotion with a flukey, shinned goal in the last minute of extra time at Wembley by Claridge and then within a few years won the League Cup and qualified for Europe.

So it was pretty gut-wrenching to lose that semi-final because not only did we miss out on Wembley, it wrecked our chances of winning promotion. The following season was all about getting the club ready to leave the Victoria Ground for the new stadium being built on the hill. We had an average season and from Christmas onwards all the talk was about how I was leaving. Clubs were supposed to be putting bids in for me of £1m, £2m or £3m, but I knew nothing. People thought it unsettled me, but I felt it was such a farcical situation and I even remember Macari asking me after a game when I was in the showers if I was on my way to QPR. And I just shrugged and said, "You're the manager. Have you accepted a bid for me?" But he didn't know and it was all cloak and dagger stuff which I was too naïve at the time to understand, but at the end of the day they wanted to pay for the stadium and both myself and Andy Griffin were sold to fund Stoke's share of the cost.

It was a shame because I was flying and scoring goals for fun. I scored five goals in the first four games at the start of that season. I'd actually got 19 goals by Christmas. I look at the stats now and think, "god, that was awesome!" I was in this team that was playing to my strengths and it was such a good time from a personal point of view. And these teams wanted me because I was performing well, which made me feel good. But then I got an injury problem, which affected me for the whole of the rest of the season. I struggled to get on to the pitch at times.

I did score a couple of goals in the Stoke v Vale derby at the end of the season as we finished in mid-table. One of those goals was a shot from the edge of the area that took a huge deflection off a defender's bum, but you have to take every goal that comes your way!

I wanted to be a part of the move to the new ground, but Stoke didn't offer me a new contract and I just went along with it as I thought they didn't want me, so I thought, "I'll find someone who does." It really disappointed me. The club were saying one thing publicly while plotting my transfer behind the scenes and it turned the fans against me. Maybe I should have been a lot stronger and admitted what was going on behind the scenes, but I think I was just a young lad and I chose the wrong path. I wish now I hadn't left. I never found the great times we had at Stoke in my career again which was depressing.

But I don't think about those times in my Stoke career. I like to remember standing in front of the Boothen End, arms both aloft and with this sea of ecstatic faces jumping up and down after my goal against Charlton. That was the time for me. That was the moment.